The Novel in the Americas

The Novel in the Americas

RAYMOND LESLIE WILLIAMS, *Editor*

UNIVERSITY PRESS OF COLORADO

Copyright © 1992 by the University Press of Colorado
P.O. Box 849
Niwot, Colorado 80544

10 9 8 7 6 5 4 3 2 1

The University Press of Colorado is a cooperative publishing enterprise supported, in part, by Adams State College, Colorado State University, Fort Lewis College, Mesa State College, Metropolitan State College of Denver, University of Colorado, University of Northern Colorado, University of Southern Colorado, and Western State College.

Library of Congress Cataloging-in-Publication Data

The Novel in the Americas / Raymond Leslie Williams, editor.
     p.   cm.
    Includes bibliographical references and index.
    ISBN 0-87081-271-8
    1. Fiction — History and criticism.   2. American fiction — History and criticism.   3. Spanish-American fiction — History and criticism.   I. Williams, Raymond L.
PN3321.N59   1992
809.3 — dc20   92-26248
                                                                       CIP

The paper used in this publication meets the minimum requirements of the American National Standard for Information Sciences—Permanence of Paper for Printed Library Materials. ANSI Z39.48–1984

∞

The Critical Studies of the Americas Committee is privileged to inaugurate its new interdisciplinary book series with this collection of essays by and about eminent writers and scholars of the Americas. It is the first of what we hope will be a set of studies that will provide an intellectual framework for critical inquiry into and initiate a hemisphericwide dialog on the interrelated societies, histories, and cultures of the Americas, North and South.

WILLIAM WEI
Managing Editor
Boulder, Colorado

In memory of Manuel Puig

Contents

Contributors

Carlos Fuentes has been a leading Mexican novelist, playwright, and essayist prominent in Latin America since the "boom" of the Latin American novel in the 1960s. Among the twenty-one books he has published, which have been translated into numerous languages, his major novels include *Where the Air Is Clear*, *The Death of Artemio Cruz*, *Aura*, *Change of Skin*, *Terra Nostra*, *The Old Gringo*, *Distant Relations*, and *The Campaign*. Fuentes has served as ambassador to France and is the recipient of both the Rómulo Gallegos Prize and the Cervantes Prize. He participated in the first and fourth Novel of the Americas symposia in 1989 and 1992.

Maxine Hong Kingston is one of the most prominent Asian-American writers today. She has published essays, reviews, and novels, including *The Woman Warrior*, *China Men*, and *Tripmaster Monkey: His Fake Book*, and has taught creative writing at the Mid-Pacific Institute and the University of Hawaii. Hong Kingston participated in the third and fourth Novel of the Americas symposia in 1990 and 1992.

William H. Gass is the David May Distinguished University Professor in the Humanities at Washington University in St. Louis, where he teaches literature and philosophy. He has published novels, short fiction, literary and philosophical essays, and poetry. Gass is the recipient of, among other awards, the Guggenheim Foundation Grant for Fiction and the Pushcart Prize and has been elected to the American Academy and Institute of Arts and Letters. His books include *Willie Masters' Lonesome Wife*, *In the Heart of the Heart of the Country*, and *The Habitations of the Word*. He participated in the third and fourth Novel of the Americas symposia in 1990 and 1992.

Raymond D. Souza is professor of Latin American literature at the University of Kansas. An authority on both Caribbean and Latin American literature, his books include *Major Cuban Novelists*, *José Lezama Lima*, *Lino Novás Calvo*, and *La historia en la narrativa hispanoamericana*.

Souza participated in the third and fourth Novel of the Americas symposia in 1990 and 1992.

Larry McCaffery is professor of English at San Diego State University. He specializes in contemporary fiction, about which he has published numerous articles, and is editor-in-chief of *Fiction International*. Some of his books include *Anything Can Happen: Interviews with Contemporary American Novelists*; *The Metafictional Muse: The Works of Robert Coover, Donald Barthelme and William Gass*; and *Postmodern Fiction: A Bio Bibliographical Guide*. He participated in the first and fourth Novel of the Americas symposia in 1989 and 1992.

John S. Brushwood is the Roberts Professor of Latin American Literature at the University of Kansas. He is the author of *Mexico in Its Novel: A Nation's Search for Identity*, *The Spanish American Novel: A Twentieth-Century Survey*, *Genteel Barbarism: New Readings of Nineteenth-Century Spanish-American Novels*, *La novela mexicana (1967–1982)*, and other books and articles on the literatures of Mexico and other Latin American countries. He participated in the third and fourth Novel of the Americas symposia in 1990 and 1992.

Federico Patán is professor of comparative literature at the National University of Mexico (UNAM). He writes weekly book reviews on Mexican literature for *Uno Más Uno* in Mexico City, and his fiction includes *En esta casa*; *Nena, me llamo Walter*; and *Ultimo exilio*. Patán participated in the first and fourth Novel of the Americas symposia in 1989 and 1992.

Davíd Carrasco teaches in the Department of Religious Studies and is director of the Mesoamerican Archive at the University of Colorado at Boulder. Among the books he has published are *Quetzalcoatal and the Irony of Empire: Myths and Prophecies in the Aztec Tradition* and *Religions of Mesoamerica*. He has also written numerous articles on Mesoamerican religions and the history of religions. Carrasco participated in the first, second, and fourth Novel of the Americas symposia in 1989, 1990, and 1992.

Raymond Leslie Williams is professor of Latin American literature at the University of Colorado at Boulder. He specializes in contemporary Latin American fiction and is editor of the *Revista de Estudios Colombianos y Latinoamericanos*. His books include *Una década de la novela* *colombiana, Gabriel García Márquez, Mario Vargas Llosa,* and *The Colombian Novel, 1844–1987.* He is the director of the Novel of the Americas Project and co-organizer of the symposia.

Ronald Sukenick teaches in the Department of English and the Creative Writing Program at the University of Colorado at Boulder and edits *The American Book Review.* His fiction — some of which has been translated into French — includes *Blown Away, Long Talking Bad Condition Blues, 98.6,* and *Endless Short Story.* He has published the essays *In Form, Down and In,* and *Wallace Stevens: Musing the Obscure.* Sukenick is co-organizer of the Novel of the Americas symposia and has participated in the four conferences.

Rikki Ducornet is novelist in residence at the University of Denver. She was born in New York and has lived in North Africa, Latin America, Canada, and France. In 1988 Ducornet was a Fellow at Radcliffe College's Bunting Institute and a recipient of a grant from the Ingram Merrill Foundation. In 1989 both her sixth volume of poetry, *The Cult of Seizure,* and her novel, *The Fountains of Neptune,* were published. *The Fountains of Neptune* is the third in a tetralogy that includes *Entering the Fire* and *The Stain.* Also in 1989 Ducornet was awarded a grant from the Eben Demarest Trust toward the completion of her fourth novel, *The Jade Cabinet.* She has participated in all four Novel of the Americas symposia.

Diamela Eltit is a Chilean writer and essayist belonging to a generation of young intellectuals who remained in Chile during the dictatorship of Augusto Pinochet and organized different kinds of resistance. The group was also involved with a variety of oppositional artistic expressions. Eltit's four novels are *Lumpérica, Por la patria, El cuarto mundo,* and *Vaca sagrada,* the transcription of a monolog of a street person in Santiago. She was the keynote speaker for the 1991 Andean Summit at the University of Colorado at Boulder, which was co-sponsored by the Novel of the Americas Project.

Fletcher Fairey is a teacher of Spanish in Chapel Hill, North Carolina. He was a graduate student at the University of Colorado at Boulder when he interviewed Mario Vargas Llosa in April 1991.

Mario Vargas Llosa is a Peruvian novelist, essayist, and playwright. He has received numerous prizes, including the Rómulo Gallegos Prize and the Ritz Hemingway Prize. His novels include *The Time of the Hero, The*

Green House, Conversation in the Cathedral, Aunt Julia and the Script Writer, The War of the End of the World, and *In Praise of the Stepmother.* He lectured at the University of Colorado at Boulder in April 1991, a lecture co-sponsored by the Novel of the Americas Project.

Preface

Every writer names the world. But the Latin American writer has been possessed by the urgency to discover; if I do not name, no one will.
— Carlos Fuentes

These words of Carlos Fuentes' were delivered in a lecture on September 25, 1992, to close the 1992 Novel of the Americas Symposium held at the University of Colorado at Boulder. Fuentes and a host of other distinguished writers and scholars have been possessed by the "urgency to discover" — perhaps even more intensely at this quincentennial moment — and the equally "possessed" Critical Studies of the Americas Committee of the University of Colorado at Boulder has spent four years organizing this inter-American dialog on the novel and the cultures of the Americas. Fuentes agreed to open the dialog in Colorado in the fall of 1989 in the form of the first plenary session of our 1989 Novel of the Americas Symposium and to close it with the final plenary session of our fourth and culminating 1992 symposium. Over 100 intellectuals have been engaged in this ongoing dialog on the cultures of the Americas, including Nicole Brossard, Maryse Condé, Henry Louis Gates, Jr., Roberto González Echevarría, Rolando Hinojosa, Linda Hogan, Linda Hutcheon, Fredric Jameson, Steve Katz, John Kronik, George Lamming, Paule Marshall, Daniel Maximin, Michael Ondaatje, Elena Poniatowska, Luis Arturo Ramos, Luis Rafael Sánchez, Severo Sarduy, Antonio Skármeta, Wolé Soyinka, Ronald Sukenick, Amy Tan, and Jane Urquhart.

Fuentes and a dozen other renowned thinkers contribute their ideas on writing in the Americas in this volume. Beyond this most generic commonality of theme, several other notable threads tie the volume together, including positions on the role of imagination, referentiality, and discussions of the modern and postmodern in the Americas. The contributors are an impressive group of seasoned intellectuals, most of whom seem to have read Jorge Luis Borges early on, and Thomas Pynchon, John Barth, Italo Calvino, and Gabriel García Márquez along the way. This commonality of background and interests unifies the volume.

All of the contributors know at least one national culture of the Americas with impressive depth. Nevertheless, none of them places much faith in the novel written or read exclusively as an expression of national or regional boundaries: as Fuentes points out in his essay, the novel today has fulfilled Johann Wolfgang von Goethe's dream and is no longer associated with a nationality or a language. Maxine Hong Kingston expresses a similar dream in her proposal for a global novel. Even I, who have made a career writing mostly about Colombian literature, must agree with Fuentes that we read García Márquez not because he writes in Spanish (and *One Hundred Years of Solitude* was written in a very Colombian Spanish), but because of his imagination.

Fuentes, who was unquestionably the major intellectual spokesperson for the "boom" of the Latin American novel in the 1960s, takes an important position in his essay vis-à-vis what might be called the postmodern condition of the Americas at the quincentennial moment. In contrast to the postmodern propositions of Jean Baudrillard and Jean-François Lyotard — positions so many First World academics have already canonized — Fuentes offers a Third World alternative. Rather than accepting at face value Baudrillard's vision of contemporary society as simulation and Lyotard's proposition on the disappearance of the grand narrative, the always combative Fuentes asks why the end of "metanarratives" does not "announce the multiplication of 'multinarratives' coming from a multiracial and polycultural universe, beyond the exclusive dominion of Western modernity."

Another factor that unifies this volume, in virtually every essay, is its reaffirmation of the author's right of invention. Several decades ago Franz Kafka and Borges seemingly disposed of the problem so impressively that they convinced a nineteen-year-old García Márquez in the late 1940s that if literature's invention could allow people to be transformed into insects on the very first page of a novel, then this Colombian wanted to be a writer. But somehow these important lessons of Borges and Kafka either have been forgotten or have not yet fully gained the acceptance in our culture that they would seem to have merited long ago. Fuentes purposely offends the mimesis police by stating unequivocally that "the novel not only reflects reality, but in effect creates a new reality." Without invention, according to Fuentes, we remain incomplete: "Imagination and language, memory and desire, are the meeting place of our incomplete humanity." Hong Kingston takes essentially the same position when she asks whether it is better to restore our cities or to rethink them. Her proposal for a global novel is essentially Borgesian and Kafkian: she asks for a work that not only goes beyond national boundaries but freely invents heretofore unimagined possibilities for human existence. For Mario Vargas Llosa, the weakness of D. H. Lawrence was that he was not inventive enough, and the novel in general "must be the product of fantasy, imagination, and obsessions."

Much contemporary fiction of the Americas seems to be following this path of invention proposed by Borges, Fuentes, Vargas Llosa, and Hong Kingston, according to John S. Brushwood and Larry McCaffery. Speaking of the situation in Mexico, Brushwood refers to Borges as one of the greatest storytellers of all time, a major influence in the renaissance of plot invention in Latin America. Brushwood's explanation of the inventive enterprise initiated by Marcel Proust is that from the time of Proust to the present, we may observe a new reality, a new perception of reality, and a new way of expressing it. Brushwood recognizes the importance of this modernist enterprise, which Erich Auerbach feared in the early part of our century but which has been the backbone of Mexican fiction of the past decades, even though many contemporary readers face this hermetic fiction with some of the doubts and reservations Auerbach expressed. McCaffery makes similar observations about the United States. In his assessment of contemporary fiction in North America, McCaffery points out how the freedom to invent, the affirmation that "all is permitted" and that fiction be "open-ended," have been virtual doctrine for North American writers of the past few decades. Similarly, Davíd Carrasco concludes that imagination is the most dynamic element in Fuentes' *The Old Gringo*.

This free invention has resulted in a crisis of representation in the contemporary novel of the Americas. Several of these writers and critics, including Fuentes, William H. Gass, Ronald Sukenick, and Rikki Ducornet, discuss the crisis. For Fuentes, the writer is a discoverer who gives a "verbal reality to the unwritten part of the world," which is always "greater than the written part." The novel "not only reflects reality, but in effect creates a new reality," as Fuentes explains. Gass does not believe in mimetic representation in fiction — or even in contemporary reality: "How easy for Jane Austen to represent the real when it was real." Any fabrication of the imagination can be a kind of writing as long as it is not representational, according to Sukenick. He also claims that "Plato was right — representation is taboo." The Cuban-Canadian-American writer Rikki Ducornet makes the following unequivocal affirmation: "I insist: it is not only our right, but our responsibility to follow our imaginations' enchanted paths wherever they would lead us; to heed those voices which inhabit our most secret (and sacred) spaces."

The insidious influence of mass media and media culture is a phenomenon that concerns McCaffery, Gass, Diamela Eltit, and Fuentes. McCaffery speaks of fiction written to a generation of readers reared in the Media Age, in which just a flick of the switch will bring them encounters with Ronald Reagan, Madonna, and *Voyager* photographs of Neptune — all brought together as equals on the flattened screens of their televisions. These new realities have begun to replace what used to be called "the real," according to some theorists of the postmodern such as Baudrillard and Lyotard. Gass portrays modern cultures totally dominated by the media, describing a commercial "pidgin culture." In Gass' vision of postmodern culture, "The last of the gods was long ago consumed. The last of the Mohicans became a novel, then a film. The last of the avant-garde is diet." Fuentes expresses concern over cultures of the Americas in which we learn more and more from the media and read less than ever.

Eltit and Fuentes also question the social conditions in which the mass media reign in Latin America. Eltit sees consumer society invading Latin America with the potential of an "eroticism of consumption." Media society creates the social body, according to Eltit. Fuentes, however, offers an alternative to those who believe that the mass media have destroyed all sense of the real and of truth. Proposing a "multinarrative" coming from a multiracial and polycultural universe, Fuentes suggests that the future should lie in "polynarratives" of liberation, which are to be found not only in the West but also in writing from Africa, Asia, and, of course, Latin America. Vargas Llosa also speaks of the "pluralistic vision of problems" that the novelist must have.

In a cultural setting where diversity is so marked and so important, as Fuentes, Eltit, and McCaffery point out, it is logical that the Americas are the scenario for multiracial and minority subgenres. In my own essay, I outline feminist projects being effected in Brazil, Colombia, Chile, and Argentina. Women writers strive toward a new feminist work; concurrently, a Jewish-American writer such as Ronald Sukenick suggests that some writers are heading toward a notion that might be called talmudic fiction. McCaffery describes a North American scene where the different multicultural and minority writers — gays, blacks, Native Americans, and others — are developing their own subgenres.

Referring to Fuentes' own fiction, Brushwood states that Fuentes is obsessed with history, and Davíd Carrasco illuminates the importance of history in *The Old Gringo*. Carrasco sees the title character in the novel as attempting to liberate himself from the fatality of history. Carrasco argues that the essence of this novel is the spectacle of border crossings between "the conscious and the unconscious minds, history and imagination." Federico Patán agrees with Brushwood and Carrasco about the importance of history for Fuentes but points out that history has been of increasing importance in Mexican fiction in general. Raymond D. Souza and Eltit would argue that history permeates Latin American fiction in general.

Indeed, Souza reads three historical fictions written in Argentina, Cuba, and the United States in order to compare their narrativization of history and their fictionalization of Christopher Columbus. He demonstrates how the Argentinean Abel Posse communicates an "interconnected vision of history," while at the same time writing a parody of historical narrative. Given the importance of history for Latin American intellectuals, it is logical for Souza to find that the past casts a longer shadow in the texts of Posse and the Cuban Alejo Carpentier than in those of the North American Stephen Marlowe. Souza observes that these texts are an "indication of the burden of the search for a redemption from history" and concludes that these three authors of the Americas represent various manifestations of the impulse to moralize events.

The future of the cultures of the Americas and their novel is a matter of interest to several of these writers. Fuentes envisions a twenty-first century defined more by variety than monotony, more by diversity than unity. He also affirms that "our literature to come, in the twenty-first century, will have learned the lessons of the past, making them present: literature does not exhaust itself in its political or historical context; it constantly opens new horizons of readership for readers that did not exist at the moment when the work was written." Gass is far more sanguine about the state of First World culture and its relationship to the future: "Our day is never yesterday; it is always tomorrow." Quoting Severo Sarduy (who participated in our Third Novel of the Americas Symposium in October 1990), Gass also speaks of one possible

novel of the future in which language will be present as the space of the
act of encoding, as a surface of unlimited transformations. Hong Kingston agrees more with the future vision of Fuentes, stating that the
novelist should forget territory, mate and mix with "exotic peoples," and
create "the new humane being."

The Quincentennial has brought many writers and scholars of the
Americas to reflect on the construct of "discovery," including Fuentes,
Gass, and Souza. Fuentes and Gass are more committed to the powers
of the imagination and the word than to the events of 1492, whatever
they were. Weaving in and out of the geographical and literary terrains
of the Americas, Gass suggests that he, and we, have been traveling in
the envelope of an image, pretending to be Columbus. When Gass does
refer to the historical Columbus, he writes him off: "Columbus' motives
were base, his plans misguided, actions ambiguous, results misconstrued;
yet this may be the usual pattern of discovery, whether exploratory or
creative, whether we want to claim a country, write the world down, or
paint its face." According to Souza, the representation of Columbus by
Posse, Carpentier, and Marlowe coincides with the pattern of discovery
outlined by Gass.

These essays were written in different contexts for a series of Novel
of the Americas symposia and for other dialogs on and off the campus
of the University of Colorado at Boulder. Nevertheless, when read as a
whole, they suggest several problems that cross many of the real and
imaginary borders of the Americas. In a way, most of these problems
have to do with the survival of the novel in the Americas and beyond.
In Fuentes' opening essay, he mentions how he first heard of the "death
of the novel" in the early 1950s — precisely during the period when he
decided to become a novelist. The novel, the bearer of novelties, was
supposedly suffering the threat of extinction in the face of the new
media. Reflecting on this adolescent horror he suffered, Fuentes makes
his defense of the imaginative power of the novel over the media. Living
in the culture of novelty that we inhabit in 1992, it is difficult to
imagine just how intimidated these nineteenth-century readers, such
as Auerbach, were at the beginning of the twentieth. We've been talking
about the efficacy of literary pyrotechnics ever since.

Formal innovation in the fiction of the Americas still remains a
problematic issue, but the terms have changed considerably since
Auerbach was confused reading James Joyce. Sukenick states that he
likes the creative methods of Raymond Roussel, but he rejects the very

same methods of Roussel's followers in the contemporary Oulipo group, for Roussel used arbitrary methods of composition to free himself from the conventional, whereas Oulipo did not. Observing how methods similar to those of Sukenick, Roussel, and the Oulipo group were practiced in Mexico in the 1970s, Brushwood explains that they resulted in a fiction that is not only fascinating and intellectually stimulating but also "hard to read" and "elitist." Brushwood claims that such extreme technical innovation in the Mexican fiction of the 1970s may have delighted a small group of readers, but it pushed a larger number into reading nonfiction. All of this rings a little of the "novel is dead" syndrome we have been suffering since Joyce — interestingly enough, exactly at the time when Joyce's impact was most felt in Latin America (since the late 1960s). Vargas Llosa states in his interview that "Joyce was nothing less than a genius." By the late 1970s, technical innovation itself had become a cliché for Latin American fiction. Consequently, the feminist projects of writers such as Eltit became quite notable in the 1980s, for her innovation has significant ideological consequences.

Five hundred years after Columbus began telling stories about the Americas, these twelve intellectuals portray a scene for the novel of the Americas that is sometimes disturbing. The novelists themselves seem almost uniformly under siege by the Media Age. Gass resigns himself to accepting the "pidgin culture" that the media and the multinationals create; Eltit sees the mass media as an object of analysis; Fuentes asserts that the imagination can be more real than the reality of modern media. As the United States suffers its 1992 recession and the Latin American nations face hyperinflation as well as massive unemployment, Fuentes contemplates the depressing image of a Mexican boy, a grade school dropout, who juggles balls to make money at the intersection of Insurgentes and Reforma in Mexico City. Fuentes laments that the boy's economic crisis has made him not just another of the growing number of illiterates in the Americas, but, much worse, "a lost reader of Juan Rulfo." Of all the problems faced by the novelists and the novel of the Americas, the problematics of the juggling boy at Insurgentes and Reforma are certainly most poignant and perhaps the most significant.

*   *   *

The essays that follow are almost all related to the four Novel of the Americas symposia that took place on the campus of the University of Colorado at Boulder between September 1989 and September 1992. Carlos Fuentes opened our activity with his keynote lecture for the first symposium in 1989, and was joined by Henry Louis Gates, Jr., Paule Marshall, Antonio Skármeta, and twenty other writers and scholars of the Americas. (Davíd Carrasco presented his "first reading" of *The Old Gringo* at this conference, a reading that he developed further for the present volume.) Our Second Novel of the Americas Symposium, held in April 1990, was opened by Ishmael Reed and closed by Michael Ondaatje, with the participation of Elena Poniatowska, Fredric Jameson, and fifteen other intellectuals. (Ronald Sukenick began some discussions at this forum that resulted in his paper "Unwriting.") William H. Gass opened our third symposium in October 1990 with his lecture "The Last of the Avant-Garde." Gass was joined by Maxine Hong Kingston, Severo Sarduy, Roberto Gonzalez Echevarría, John Kronik, John S. Brushwood, Daniel Maximin, Luis Arturo Ramos, Rikki Ducornet, and others. (Rikki Ducornet gave her "Manifesto in Voices" at this symposium.)

The article by Fuentes and the existence of this volume are the result of some very special circumstances. In the fall of 1989, when Fuentes spoke at our first symposium, he agreed to return in 1992. In the spring of 1991, he agreed to write his closing lecture in advance so that it could appear in this volume. Fuentes called me from Santiago de Chile in December 1991, indicating that he had begun his essay and that he would complete it in Mexico City by the end of the month. I went to Mexico City (with the dozen texts for this volume in my suitcase) on January 3, 1992. The next day Carlos invited me to his home and gave me what I like to call "the last manuscript of the Americas." I say this because the sheets of paper that Fuentes gave me in his home in the colonial neighborhood of San Gerónimo that Saturday afternoon indeed constituted a "manuscript" — composed on a typewriter with copious insertions and changes scribed by hand. Nowadays Gabriel García Márquez, Mario Vargas Llosa, Maxine Hong Kingston, and virtually every other novelist in the Americas (at least among those whom I know) writes with a word processor. (Ronald Sukenick gave me a disk for his "Unwriting" in December 1991; Diamela Eltit printed her piece from her word processor on January 6, 1992; Davíd Carrasco had to send his late because he couldn't find a printer for his program at Princeton, where he was visiting.)

With "the last manuscript of the Americas" in my possession, I returned to the Hotel María Cristina in downtown Mexico City (about three blocks from the juggling boy at Insurgentes and Reforma), where I read Fuentes' "Latin America and the Universality of the Novel." I realized, of course, that I had an outstanding essay in my hands. As editor of this volume, however, I was even more fascinated and excited as I began to discover numerous connections unfolding before my eyes: Fuentes' piece was an invitation to find associations among the cultures of the Americas, as well as among the dozen other essays I had been perusing on the flight from Colorado to Mexico.

*   *   *

I would like to express my appreciation to the numerous individuals and institutions who have made these four Novel of the Americas symposia and this volume possible, in addition to Carlos Fuentes. Vice-Chancellor Bruce Ekstrand of the University of Colorado at Boulder launched the idea of Critical Studies of the Americas on our campus and supported our activity unstintingly. We also enjoyed the timely support of our chancellor, James Corbridge, and the dean of the College of Arts and Sciences, Charles Middleton. The idea for the Novel of the Americas symposia was born in April 1989, when Ronald Sukenick and I found ourselves talking regularly about the connections between North American and Latin American fiction, conversations that arose during the visits of Manuel Puig and Luis Rafael Sánchez. Perhaps that was the moment when we too were possessed by the "urgency to discover." When I asked Puig and Sánchez their opinion of this project, they both responded enthusiastically and agreed to return in 1992. John Kronik was also with us that spring, visiting from Cornell, and he too offered encouragement and sound advice as we conceived this project. By the end of the month, Sukenick and I, with the support of the Critical Studies of the Americas Committee, decided to launch this ongoing North-South dialog. We have enjoyed the support of numerous colleagues on campus, particularly Cordelia Candelaria, Manning Marable, Warren Motte, Steven Katz, Linda Hogan, Marilyn Krysl, David Simpson, Georgyana Colvile, Salvador Rodriguez del Pino, Howard Goldblatt, Ann Scarboro, Robin Jones, Lorna Dee Cervantes, Evelyn Hu-Dehart, and Peter Michelson. The Graduate Committee for Arts and Humanities as well as the Department of English and the Department of Spanish and Portuguese have been important contributors. Anne Waldman, director of the Naropa Institute, and Stuart Hughes of the Canadian Consulate in San Francisco have also been appreciated supporters.

Finally, I would like to thank three individuals whose assistance in the Novel of the Americas symposia and in preparing this volume has been invaluable: Terri Mason, Michael Buzan, and Guillermo García-Corales. Without them, the essay by Fuentes, and the presence of Manuel Puig on our campus in April 1989, none of this would have been possible.

RAYMOND LESLIE WILLIAMS

The Novel in the Americas

Latin America and the Universality of the Novel

CARLOS FUENTES, *Mexico City, Mexico*

Every writer names the world. But the Latin American writer has been possessed by the urgency to discover: if I do not name, no one will; if I do not write, all shall be forgotten; and if all is forgotten, we shall cease to exist. This urgency — even this fear — has forced the writers in our countries, quite often, to act as legislators, labor leaders, statesmen, journalists, and even redeemers of their societies. This was due, in great measure, to the absence or weakness of the above-mentioned functions in our traditionally feeble civil societies.

This demand gave rise to much bad literature in Latin America. Many novels written to save the miner or the peasant saved neither them nor literature. The workers will only save themselves through political action. Literature, instead, understood that its function would not be effective in purely political terms but, rather, to the degree to which the writer can affect social values at the level of the communicability of the imagination and the strengthening of the language.

Our modern literature thus created its own tradition: that of uniting, instead of separating, the aesthetic and political components of the literary task. We have been able, by and large, to admit into our works both the city and the art; we have been able to unite, instead of separating, the state of the art and the state of the city.

Our city, our Latin American polis, is in crisis, and the writer can no longer respond to it by substituting functions that the society, ever stronger and more diversified, has now taken upon itself. The negative side of this crisis is well known to all of you: hyperinflation and unemployment; growing poverty and sickness; diminishing salaries, savings, and productivity; and fragile democratic institutions menaced by the crisis of the four Ds: debt, development, drugs, and democracy. The positive side is that, beyond the traditional, overcentralized institutions of Army, Church, State and even political parties, civil society has strengthened itself by taking on multiple initiatives from the bottom and from the periphery, discovering in the midst of our economic and political failures the saving grace of the continuity of the culture. It has also discovered that the culture is made by all of us, its creators and then its bearers, the citizens; and that our past failure, but also our present task, is to translate the continuity of the culture and the energy of the society to the economic and political institutions at present widely divergent from their cultural sources.

The writer then appears on the political scene as a citizen with political options, no more, and no less, than other professionals or workers within the society. Yet the writers' distinction is that their work directly affects the verbal imagination and, within this sphere, their mission is not very different from that of writers in other cultures.

Undoubtedly, the crisis has created precise and difficult conditions for writers and for readers throughout Latin America. The readers of Latin American literature are, above all, young men and women between the ages of fifteen and twenty-five, in a continent of 400 million people, where half the population is eighteen years old or less. Our young people acquire a taste for culture by reading, at an early age, the works of Pablo Neruda or Jorge Luis Borges. But the high prices of books today, along with the declining purchasing power of most middle-class readers, threaten us all with a disruption of the circle that we have, with very great effort, drawn during the past fifty years: the circle that goes from writer to publisher to distributor to bookseller to reader, and back to writer.

Buying and reading books has been more than a status symbol in modern Latin America: books are the effective tool by which, in a society of rising expectations, the child of the working class establishes his or her stake in a more just and democratic society, and claims the chance to reach high school and even university levels. That hope is broken today. Young men and women who once had the opportunity of studying until age fifteen and beyond must now leave their education at age ten or eleven so as to work and bring money home; instead of students and readers, they become street-corner hawkers or public square jugglers, or they join violent gangs. Often, they are murdered by adults fearful of their teenage potential for crime.

And yet this little boy with a clown's red nose, juggling balls on the corner of Insurgentes and Reforma in Mexico City, is really a lost reader of Juan Rulfo, and that young man brutally murdered in a *favela* in Rio de Janeiro could have been a reader of Guimaraes Rosa.

The readers are there, nevertheless, potential and latent — as potential as the very quick growth of our population, as latent as the very possibility that out of this deep crisis, Latin America might emerge, chastised and strengthened, demanding nothing less than renewed growth with social justice and political democracy. No less.

But whatever the outcome of our present dilemmas, the writers will not reach the readers by cheapening their own communication and succumbing to the fallacy that by lowering standards, they will gain a wider public. This is perhaps true in a very transitory way: a best-seller can be easily fabricated. The recipes are there, and the reader for any sort of potboiler is foreseeable. But even if *Gone With the Wind* can make a spectacular comeback, I defy anyone to remember or read the best-selling novel of 1933 — Hervey Allen's *Anthony Adverse*.

This leads me to the second issue that — directly dependent on the accessibility of readership — faces the novel in Latin America, Europe, or the United States, which is the seemingly unbeatable challenge of the other means of information, basically the media and entertainment. I remember how depressed I felt when I began writing in the 1950s and all I heard around me were the ominous words: "The novel is dead." And it is dead, it was added, because it cannot compete with radio, film, TV, journalism, which have annexed territories traditionally occupied by the novel, whose very name, *novella*, bearer of novelties, is mocked and erased by the modern means of instant communication. Furthermore — we were given no quarter — the novel cannot compete, as a vehicle of information, with any book on psychology, economics, or history. But then, is not this the *quid*? Even if we are talking of information, are we not truly referring to knowledge — unless we wish to admit that, sometimes, information is separated from knowledge or reduced to a sickly state of mere, unknowing novelty, sans even information?

I believe that the novelists of my generation, not only in Latin America, but throughout the world, came to understand, in the face of the challenge of the massive means of modern information, that the novel does not inform: it imagines, and that in literature, the name of knowledge is imagination. But again, does this not merely sanction the fact that readers abandon literature by the droves — perhaps, by the herds — and that, if we want to recapture readership, we must become more accessible, more entertaining, or, as the unwittingly revealing adjective in current Spanish journalism has it, "lighter"?

Not long ago, the distinguished Spanish novelist José María Guelbenzu skillfully rejected the fashionable desire for "light" or "amusing" literature by reminding each and all that literature is indeed elitist in its solitary corner of creation, fed by dreams, fears, ghosts, confessions, desires, humors. What *should* be democratic, says Guelbenzu, is not the act of creating literature, but the act of acceding to literature, and this — I quote him — can only "be obtained . . . through an education that truly combats ignorance." He also reminds us that democracy cannot be identified with sloth, mediocrity, or ignorance. On the contrary, to be fully democratic means to display a high degree of education and a demanding lucidity. That is, the democratic reader should be an educated, well-informed, and exigent reader, whose reading in this way would become an act parallel to that of the literary creation itself: a reading every inch as creative as writing. To identify literature with "democratic" popularity is to demean both literature and democracy. And, in the long run, if you wound creativity, you end up by killing democracy.

Sometimes, in Latin America, it has been said that novels such as Lezama Lima's *Paradiso* or Cortázar's *Hopscotch* cannot be received by an illiterate or semiliterate public. My response has always been: what will our illiterates read when they cease to be illiterate? *Superman* or *Don Quixote*? Shakespeare or *Hola!* magazine? The hope of a Lezama Lima or a Cortázar in Latin America is that of a Guelbenzu in Spain: novels must be entertaining, fashion says. And Guelbenzu asks himself: "Isn't the opposite more true? Is it not the reader who has to learn how to amuse himself?" After all, the powers of amusement of a novel much berated in its time, and always considered difficult — to wit, Laurence Sterne's *Tristam Shandy* — has lived and shall live longer than the combined efforts of Sidney Sheldon and Jackie Collins.

At the center of this new quarrel of the universals, we thus find the readers and two manners of inviting them to participate in any given work of literature. One is the way of the commercial best-seller, which presumes the existence of an identifiable reader, whose tastes, judgments, and prejudices are known beforehand by the author, who then follows a recipe and comes forth, like a literary Julia Child, with his commercial dish. In these cases, the readers do not truly read; they are, perhaps, amused, but the fast food rapidly goes through their intestines and is then expelled through what Juan Goytisolo calls *el despeñadoro del recto*. Other works of fiction search for the as yet inexistent reader, the reader-to-be, the reader to be discovered in the very act of reading. When such a work and such a reader meet, the novel is truly born. Its permanent residence is in the hearts and minds of men and women — *in yollotl, in ixtl,* as the Aztecs used to say: the shared head and heart of Cervantes and his readers, of Stendhal, Proust, Kafka, and their readers.

When this union between the potential novel and its potential readership occurs, literature answers the question posed by the crisis of the novel in a world dominated by the media: what *can* the novel say that *cannot* be said otherwise? It is the radical question of Hermann Broch, and it is concretely answered by a constellation of novelists such as the world has rarely known. No longer associated only with a nationality or even a language, they perhaps have made Goethe's dream of a world literature come true: Günter Grass, Nadine Gordimer, Joan Didion, Julián Rios, Severo Sarduy, Chinua Acheebe, Italo Calvino, Juan Goytisolo, Toni Morrison, Margaret Atwood, Sonallah Ibrahim, and George Konrad somehow transcend the previous limitations of nationalism: no one reads Milan Kundera because he is Czech, or García Márquez because he writes in Spanish; they are read because of the quality of their imaginations.

But how are these imaginations displayed? What do these novels say that cannot be said in any other way?

I would answer, first, by saying that they give verbal reality to the unwritten part of the world, which will always be far greater than the written part. And in this sense, to be sure, all writers share the fundamental fear of the discoverer: if I do not name, no one will; if I do not say, the world will fall silent. And an unsaid or unwritten word does condemn us to death or to dearth: in Spanish, a writer can say that only what is *dicho* is *dichoso:* a silent world is a world *desdichada*. For by saying, the novel makes visible the invisible part of reality, and it does so in a way unforeseen by the realist or psychological canons of the past. In the fulsome manner imagined by Bakhtin, the contemporary novelist uses fiction as an arena where not only characters meet, but also languages, codes of behavior, distant historical eras, and multiple genres, breaking down artificial barriers and constantly enlarging the territory of the human presence in history.

Through this process, the novel not only reflects reality, but in effect *creates* a new reality, one capable of admitting new desires, social behaviors, and moral demands that might go unheeded if not touched by the knowledge of the literary imagination. And so, the novel creates a new time for its readers: the past is saved from becoming a museum, or the future an unattainable ideological promise. The novel makes of the past, memory, and of the future, desire. But both happen *today*, in the *present* of the reader who, by reading, remembers and desires. William Faulkner said it better than anyone: "All is present, you understand? Today will not end until tomorrow and tomorrow began 10,000 years ago."

Working within the vast, universal project of the contemporary novel, the Latin American writer, while sharing the burdens, dreams, and demands of novelists everywhere, does add some specific traits to this common labor. I have remarked that the novel is conscious that it not only reflects reality but creates a new, unpublished reality, or, if you wish, *adds* to reality, thus enlarging the territory of the human presence in history. Furthermore, the novel roots its historical reality in the present, where, by reading, we remember and desire. This leads me to yet another issue where the specificity of the Latin American novel holds, perhaps, more than a few lessons for the universal genre of genres we are discussing, and that is the relationship of the novel to history.

It has often, and humorously, been said that the novel in Latin America must compete with a political history more fantastic than any tale by Borges. How to compete, for example, with the Mexican dictator Antonio López de Santa Anna, eleven times president of the republic, capable of staging coups against himself, who lost his leg in combat against the French in the so-called War of the Pastries, had it buried in a cathedral with pomp and ecclesiastical blessings, saw it dragged out by the mob each time he fell from power, and, on recapturing the presidency, had it buried and blessed once more? How to compete with Juan Vicente Gómez, for thirty years president of Venezuela, who feigned his own death so as to round up and shoot those who dared to celebrate, and who, when he finally died, had to be propped up in the presidential chair, in full uniform and wearing the presidential sash, so that the people could touch him and confirm that, this time, he was *truly* dead?

How? Since in Latin America history beats fiction, fiction has tried to beat history. The response to the enormity of Santa Anna, Gómez, and the like is, as you well know, a subgenre of Latin American fiction known as "the novel of the dictator," whose granddaddy is Valle Inclán's *Tirano Banderas*, the daddy Miguel Angel Asturias' *El Señor Presidente*, and the lively, contemporary offspring Alejo Carpentier's *Reason of State*, Augusto Roa Bastos' *I the Supreme*, and Gabriel García Márquez' *The Autumn of the Patriarch*. But this would only be the tip of the narrative iceberg — and perhaps the final image of our "magical realism" is that of Chilean ships hauling an iceberg all the way from the Antarctic to the warm waters of the Guadalquivir in time for the Seville World's Fair of 1992! Fact now imitates fiction, for in *The Autumn of the Patriarch*, García Márquez' dictator sells the Caribbean Sea to an American millionaire, who promptly takes it to the Arizona desert.

More specifically, Seymour Menton of the University of California at Irvine highlights the historical vocation of the most recent Latin American novel: the reflection on the past appears as the harbinger of a narrative for the future. In this tendency that Menton has distinguished, I see an affirmation of the power of fiction to say what few historians are capable of saying: the past is not over yet; the past must be reinvented every minute so that the present will not die in our hands. I suggest that our recent historical novels be read in this spirit, be they the minute reconstruction of the brief Mexican empire of Maximilian and Charlotte by Fernando del Paso, or the melancholy voyage of Simón Bolívar's sick body, dragging his lucid mind to death on the sea that he uselessly plowed, in García Márquez.

Yet there are two less direct ways of approaching the fiction of history, and both, naturally enough, are indicated by Argentine writers. Since this is, in a way, the Latin American nation with *less* history — the old joke says that Mexicans descend from the Aztecs and Argentineans descend from the ships — perhaps no other nation has so fervently had to invent itself a history beyond history, a verbal history responding to the culture's desperate, solitary cry: please, verbalize me.

Borges, of course, is the source of this *other* historicity, which compensates for the lack of Mayan ruins, Incaic belvederes, or Toltec cosmogonies with the total space of *The Aleph*, the total time of *The Garden of Forking Paths*, or the total book of *The Library of Babel*. But just as outstanding as his invention of cities within cities, cities revealed only by the fact that other imaginary cities hide them — Tlön, Uqbarm, Orbis Tertius — is the actual creation of mythical spaces in the city of Buenos Aires, *las orillas* (margins), which Borges invented but which then became as real as the midnight London of *Our Mutual Friend* or the phantasmagoric Paris of *La fille aux yeux d'or*.

Given this capacity for creating reality through the imagination, it is not surprising that the latest generation of Argentine novelists should have gone directly to the root of the discovery and conquest of the New World, uncovering what the discovery hides, as in the novels of Abel Posse, or radicalizing to the extreme the hermetic isolation of the Indian world, as in those of Juan José Saer. Perhaps the brilliant young Argentine novelist César Aira expresses it best in his lonely quest for a nonexistent Indian culture in Argentina: "The Indians, clearly seen, were a pure absence, but made of a most exclusive quality of presence. Thus, the fear that they provoked."

History as absence: nothing better provokes, not only fear, perhaps, but the response of a creative historical imagination. That most lucid of contemporary Argentine authors, Héctor Libertella, gives the supremely ironic answer: he casts a bottle into the sea. In it are stuffed the only proofs of Ferdinand Magellan's trip around the world: the diary of Pigafetta.

History as a bottle thrown into the sea: the remote past meets the most immediate present when, in the throes of repression and dictatorship, a whole nation disappears and is only preserved in the Argentine novels of Luis Valenzuela, Daniel Moyano, and Elvira Orphée, or in the Chilean pages of Antonio Skármeta and Ariel Dorfman.

Where does Tomás Eloy Martínez' splendid *Novel of Perón* take place, then: in the immediate past of Argentina's necrophiliac politics, or in the immediate future, when the author's humor shall make the past present, bearable, and even more importantly, readable?

I am underlining the contemporary historical fiction of Latin America, and particularly that of the country that supposedly has less history, Argentina, because I suspect that this manner of fictionalizing fills a very precise need in the modern world — or, if you wish, in the postmodern world, whatever that means. After all, modernity is an endless project, perpetually unfinished. What has changed, perhaps, is the perception expressed by Jean Baudrillard that "the future has arrived, everything has arrived, everything is now here. . . ." But this, promptly adds Jean-François Lyotard, only means that the Western tradition has exhausted what he calls "the metanarratives of liberation." Yet does not the end of these "metanarratives" of enlightened modernity announce the multiplication of "multinarratives" coming from a multiracial and polycultural universe, beyond the exclusive dominion of Western modernity? The "incredulity toward metanarratives" of Western modernity can be displaced by the credulity toward the polynarratives that speak for multiple projects of liberation, not only in the West (Grass, Goytisolo, Conrad), but also in Africa (Rushdie, Desai, Bao Dai), and, certainly, in Latin America, which after all is *l'Extrème Occident*. The Western Disneyland of acedia and incredulity can perhaps receive, from the majority of humankind, a message that Baudrillard as well as Lyotard might accept: that of "activating the differences."

This activation of differences, as Lyotard calls it, is but another way of expressing that our post–Cold War world is certainly not moving toward an illusory and perhaps unwholesome unity, but toward ever greater and healthier differentiation. The novel is indeed dead if it promotes a unified, orthodox world view; it thrives on the plural, the unorthodox, the fugitive — and did not one of our greatest Baroque poets, Quevedo, write once and for all that "only what is fugitive perdures and lasts forever"? — "Sólo lo fugitivo permanece y dura."

What Bakhtin called "the narrative polyphony" is not alien to the conviction that in the coming century, whatever our sphere of activities, we shall be entering what Max Weber once called "a polytheism of values." Everything — communications, the economy, science and technology, but also ethnic demands, revived nationalisms, the return of the tribes with their idols, the coexistence of vertiginous progress with the resurrection of all that was dead — variety and not monotony, diversity more than unity, will define the culture of the coming century.

This means that we Latin Americans, at the same time that we preserve our national or regional identities, shall have to subject them to the proof of the other, the constant encounter with what we are not. But in this are we not now comparable to every single man and woman in the world? From the South to the North, from the East to the West, mass migration will be the single most important event of the twenty-first century, challenging our capacity for giving and receiving, our prejudices and our generosity as well.

As we face the born-again fascisms, anti-Semitism, anti-Arabism, anti-Latino-Americanism, exclusion and the pogrom, we ourselves must understand that an isolated identity soon perishes. An isolated culture can become folklore, mania, or specular theater. Even worse: it can weaken us irreparably through lack of competition and points of comparison. We are in the world, we live with the others, we live in history, and we shall have to respond for our memory, our desire, and our presence on earth in the name of the continuity of life.

We in Latin America cannot continue living off the meager capital of underdevelopment, but must face the challenges of a more fulsome cultural development, with all the risks, certainly, that this implies, but with the intelligence that through the "polytheism of values" Weber alludes to, the values of the civil society, which are centrifugal, decentralizing, creative, shall be strengthened and will thus strengthen our own cultural communities.

The knowledge of literature makes it more probable that we will recognize ourselves in others. Imagination and language, memory and desire, are the meeting place of our incomplete humanity. Literature teaches us that the greatest values are shared values, and that we recognize ourselves best when we recognize the other and his or her values, but that we negate and isolate ourselves when we deny or isolate the values of the other.

We Latin American novelists truly recognize ourselves in the Western other, who then becomes ours, when Italo Calvino affirms that literature is a model of values, capable of proposing scenarios of language, vision, imagination, and correlation of events. We recognize ourselves in Hans Robert Jauss when he tells us that literature anticipates possibilities as yet unrealized, broadens the space of social conduct, and opens roads for new goals, desires, and demands. We recognize ourselves in Milan Kundera, finally, when he writes that literature is a perpetual redefinition of the human being *as* problem.

All of this demands that the novel formulate itself as incessant conflict, so as to discover what has not yet been discovered, remember what has been forgotten, give voice to silence and wings to the desire of all that has been stunted by injustice, indifference, prejudice, ignorance, or hatred.

To do so, we must then see ourselves and the world as unfinished projects, as perpetually incomplete personalities, as voices that have not said their last word. To do so, we must constantly articulate a tradition and constantly push outward to possibilities of being men and women who are *in* history but also *make* history.

Latin America, this Latin America of ours in transformation, proposes no more and no less than to constantly redefine its men and women as problems, perhaps even as enigmas, but never as dogmatic responses or concluded realities. And is not this what best describes modern literature and, in particular, the novel?

The novel gains the right to criticize the world by showing, first of all, its capacity for criticizing itself. It is the criticism of the work of art by the work of art itself that reveals both the work of art and its social dimensions. Literature thus proposes the possibility of verbal imagination as a reality no less real than history itself. Literature constantly announces a new world: the imminent world. For it knows that after the terrible uncertainties and violence of our century, history has become only a possibility, never more a certitude.

The same has occurred to literature, with history, inside history, against history: literature as a countertime and a second reading of the historical. This is especially true of the novel of the Indo-Afro-Iberian New World. In order to sustain a whole historical experience, the Latin American novel has had to devour enormous slabs of history, jump over deep chasms, and consume that gigantic synthesis in the form of novels called *Hopscotch, Paradiso, One Hundred Years of Solitude, Conversation in the Cathedral, The Lost Steps, The Obscene Bird of Night, Pedro Páramo, The Devil to Pay in the Backlands,* the entire saga of Santa María by Juan Carlos Onetti, and perhaps the title that contains them all: *The Republic of Dreams* by the Brazilian Nélida Piñón.

Our literature to come, in the twenty-first century, will have learned the lessons of the past, making them present: literature does not exhaust itself in its political or historical context; it constantly opens new horizons of readership for readers who did not exist at the moment when the work was written. We know that a novel is written not only for the future, but also for the past, which it reveals today with a novelty different from that which it had yesterday.

A narrative violation of the codes of realistic certainty through hyperbole, delirium, and dream, the Latin American novel has signified the creation of another history, manifesting itself through individual writing, but also proposing the memory and the future of our communities in crisis. Name and voice, state of the art and state of the city: the movement of the Latin American novel has been parallel to that of our history, contributing to its cultural continuity. Today, it is a novel immersed in a society of deep social, political, and economic crises. But this is also, let us not forget it, a crisis that signals the appearance of critical societies, and societies in crisis due to an excessive and chaotic growth, but societies retaining, in crisis, their energy, creating a new economy, a new politics, new institutions wrought through mass movements, elections, evolution, and revolution.

To these new societies, which are now occupying larger and larger spaces in our republics, transforming them, pluralizing the traditional centers of power, the literature of Latin America is trying to respond, helping to shrink the distance between cultural reality and political institutions, giving shape to chaos, hope to desperation, direction to ideas, and communicability, truth, and beauty to the very vehicle of form, thought, and hope: that is, to language and the imagination.

The Novel's Next Step: From the Novel of the Americas to the Global Novel

MAXINE HONG KINGSTON, *Oakland, California*

I'm going to give you a head start on the book that somebody ought to be working on. The hands of the clock are minutes away from nuclear midnight. And I am slow, each book taking me longer to write. I didn't finish the story to stop the war in Vietnam until 1980. So let me set down what has to be done, and maybe hurry creation, which is about two steps ahead of destruction.

The protagonist has been born already; in fact, he's twenty-three years old and his name is Wittman Ah Sing, hero of *Tripmaster Monkey*. He has potential, having devised a "fake book" of political and artistic intentions to be improvisationally carried out. All the writer has to do is make Wittman grow up, and Huck Finn and Holden Caulfield will grow up. We need a sequel to adolescence — an idea of the humane beings that we may become. And the world would have a sequel.

How to write a novel that uses nonviolent means to get to non-violent ends? We are addicted to excitement and crisis. We confuse "pacific" and "passive," and are afraid that a world without war is a place where we'll die of boredom. A tale about a society in which characters deal with one another nonviolently seems so anomalous that we've hardly begun to invent its tactics, its drama. There's a creative-writing adage that the loaded gun in an early chapter has to go off later on. How to break that rule? The loaded guns — and the first-strike and second-strike bombs — are ready. How to not shoot and not launch, and yet have drama? The writer needs to imagine the world healthy, nurturing young Wittman to be a good man, a citizen whose work improves life.

Suppose: after gathering everybody he knows and putting on a show, as he does in *Tripmaster Monkey*, Wittman Ah Sing and his wife

This article appeared originally as "The Novel's Next Step" in *Mother Jones*, vol. 14, no. 10, Dec. 1989, pp. 37–41. Reprinted with permission.

Taña, like many Californians of the sixties, go somewhere to start a commune. They will take along Paul Goodman's *Communitas* as their field guide. A good man, a good Buddhist, builds his *sangha*. Animals have been miraculously appearing and will help deconstruct the cities. Pheasants have been spotted flying low along the streets of Detroit. In Studio City, where I lived for a while, coyotes cross Ventura Boulevard to hunt cats. We need more ideas like the junk-car reef off Honolulu; the crannies and surfaces of the sunken cars attract fish and barnacles. In British, Dutch, and Australian writing, there are stories about squatters illegally claiming empty houses and apartments. And Jimmy and Rosalynn Carter set an example of charity, repairing inner-city buildings with their own hands. (Is it better to restore cities, though, or to rethink them?)

As *Tripmaster Monkey* ends, Wittman Ah Sing decides to flee conscription. Having always lived in cities, he will not have it in him to go to the north woods and start a commune from scratch. Maybe I'll have him do what I did — go to Hawaii on the way to Japan, a country he thinks has a strong peace movement. But he stops at the verge of America. His fellow draft dodgers are lighting out for Molokai and Kauai. "Go stay Kauai, FBI man no can find 'em." Most Hawaiians, however, patriotically enlist, as the poor and the minorities have done during all the American wars. Paradise turns out to be the staging area for Vietnam. The mountains echo with target practice. Tanks go around and around Oahu, and ships loaded with rockets leave the harbor. Soldiers, bandaged on shockingly various parts of their bodies, recuperate on the beaches. The peace demonstrators are few, only about ten pacifists and Quakers; Wittman and Taña join them.

The motley people of Hawaii teach Wittman that a Chinese American is a *pake*. He studies strangers to see who his long lost relatives might be. Every family talks story about some lonely old ancestor who came across the sea and became *hanai* to them — "worked hard, that *pake*" — and took care of the entire family. Wittman identifies with Hawaiian men, who look somewhat like himself because they're part Chinese, but who are as macho physically as he is macho verbally. He is a tripping, traveling monkey and they are of the *aina*, the land, which they're losing. Vivid nature fluorescently gets through even to our city monkey. Sitting on the ground in silence with others, listening to the ocean under the night sky, he understands that the universe is made up of more silence than words. All he need do is stop talking, and he becomes one with everything and everybody else. (The silence will counterpoint the twelve-speaker blast-out in *The Fake Book*.) All of us lost land, and we migrate from country to country, vying with those who got there earlier. Forget territory. Let's make love, mate and mix with exotic peoples, and create the new humane being.

Because he has married Taña De Weese, blond and Caucasian, Wittman, who invents philosophies to catch up with his actions as well as vice versa, recommends interracial marriage as the way to integrate the planet. *Hapa* children of any combination are the most beautiful, and the Ah Sing–De Weeses adopt one. With its dark red skin and little blue-black eyes, their *hanai* baby looks like all babies, so they decide that it can be any race. Wittman, taking up the role of father, practices the principle that we ought to be able to learn to love any stranger.

There are male animals — hamsters and rabbits are two species I myself have witnessed — that have to be separated from the birthing females to stop them from eating the babies. Just so, older men, even war veterans, draft boys and send them to war. Nations have wars every generation, and kill off young men. Why is this? Why doesn't Wittman have this instinct? Doesn't he know the difference between being fatherly and being motherly?

Sometimes strangers don't like being loved. Soon after arriving in Hawaii, I worked in a community project, my portion of which was to get dropouts to drop in and learn how to read. Saul Alinsky lectured to us, "Burn it down," perhaps only quoting a slogan from Watts. The Hawaiians answered, "It's too beautiful to burn down." Then they beat up our two VISTA workers, who were blacks sent by a church in the Midwest, and ran them out of town. My next community project was Sanctuary, for AWOL soldiers. They were on R and R in paradise and did not want to go back to Vietnam. Wittman and Taña could teach reading in the front room and try to keep their two AWOLs from coming out of the back room. They'll take their kid with them and join the communal Sanctuary at the Church of the Crossroads, where everyone gathers — AWOL soldiers and sailors, servicemen's unionists, hippies, Yippies, sociologists, Quakers, Buddhists, Catholic Action, kahunas, reporters, infiltrators. Outside, the black chaplain from Schofield yells into a bullhorn for his men to give themselves up. Wittman directs the dropouts and the AWOLs in a performance of Megan Terry's *Viet Rock* that wins hearts and blows minds.

The Sanctuary in Honolulu was the latest setting up of a City of Refuge, a free zone that would give absolute security to fugitives. Such an idea has been thought up and tried by many civilizations — Phoenicians, Syrians, Greeks, Romans. Moses appointed six Levitical cities and "intaking cities," three on either side of the Jordan. Medieval and Renaissance churches were sacred precincts of asylum. On the Big Island of Hawaii, stone deities and a wall mark off a jut of land that is its City of Refuge. If the fugitive could swim or run to the City, the priests protected him or her. Mark Twain wrote about crowds lining the way to the gate, cheering on a man whose pursuers were racing to catch him. You can hide under the rock that hid Queen Ka'ahumanu, revolutionary feminist breaker of *kapu*. The City of Refuge is a desolate spot of black rock and salt water; fugitives could not have survived there without the cooperation of the community. Fictionally, it would be dramatic to set the Vietnam Sanctuary on the Big Island, but I want to tell the true history of places of peace, and how they were established during the worst of times. Sanctuary has evolved so that it can be set up in the middle of a secular city like Honolulu. Can Cities of Refuge last and grow without war conditions? Is there an Asian tradition of refugees attaining sacred ground and claiming protection by its deity? I want to follow the evolution of a humane impulse, and support the newest Sanctuary movement, harboring refugees in flight from repressive Central American regimes.

By carrying out visions of *aina* and *sangha*, Wittman, Monkey of 72 Transformations, becomes almost Hawaiian. (When he learns their music, he will be truly Hawaiian.) A human being is a thinking creature; whatever and whomever we know belong to us, and we become part of them. Learning the culture and history of the land we're living on, we take root in the earth; we have Native American ancestors. We are already part white from learning in school about pilgrims and pioneers. And we are getting better at being black because of ethnic studies and Alex Haley giving us roots. The monkey, who is able to change into fish, birds, mammals, and buildings, can now realize himself as many kinds of people. The ancestors connect us tribally and globally, and guide our evolution. We can make the planet a beneficent home for all.

The dream of the great American novel is past. We need to write the global novel. Its setting will be the United States, destination of journeys from everywhere. Wittman and Taña cut out of California only to find themselves among more Americans. Everybody gathers and regathers, unable to get away from one another until we work out how to live peacefully together. The pheasants and coyotes are among the hunters. Refugees from Southeast Asia and South America are coming to the last place that you would think North Americans would make unlivable, the United States. We shut the borders; migrants drop from the sky, as in Salman Rushdie's *The Satanic Verses*, a pioneer global novel for which the author has risked life and art. The danger is that the global novel has to imitate chaos: loaded guns, bombs, leaking boats, broken-down civilizations, a hole in the sky, broken English, people who refuse connections with others. How to stretch the novel to comprehend our times — no guarantees of inherent or eventual order — without it falling apart? How to integrate the surreal, society, our psyches?

Start with the characters. Find out — invent — how those AWOL soldiers, who came from the Midwest and the South and went to Vietnam and back, make themselves whole. And how those black VISTA workers become generous men. And how the Hawaiians save the *aina*. Another global writer, Bharati Mukherjee, wrote about a Canadian orphanage that took in mutilated children from Korea, Cambodia, Central America. One of those children, Angela — soldiers had cut off her nipples and thrown her into a pit — has turned eighteen and is about to leave the orphanage. How does she grow up a whole woman? Wittman has to break open the Chinese-American consciousness that he built with such difficulty and be a world citizen. And Taña has to use the freedom the feminists have won. These struggles have got to result in happy endings for all. And readers must learn not to worship tragedy as the highest art anymore.

For inspiring the global novel, I would read again these ancestral guides: nineteenth-century Russian novels on social experiments, the most famous being Leo Tolstoy's utopian farm at the end of *Anna Karenina*. The most entertaining were about free love; a trio loves together, each with a room of his or her own. *Sensei and His People*, by Yoshi Sugihara and David Plath, about a commune that Japanese settlers started in Manchuria in the thirties. Paul Goodman's *Making Do*, to remind us of urban conditions and humanitarian values and goals. These books keep to classical form; the problems are not so chaotic nor outcomes so revolutionary that they explode fiction. Tolstoy did not foresee technology overwhelming the land and its people. The free lovers do not go much outside the house. Sensei's commune ignores the existence of native Manchurians. And making do, scraping along, squatting and cadging, leaves too much in place. A few people living cooperatively could make repercussions that slowly change society; such a novel ought to take a long time in the reading, teaching readers to enjoy the slowness.

You have to withstand about a hundred pages of chaos in Mario Vargas Llosa's *The War of the End of the World,* which seems to be a descendant of *Water Margin,* the 800-year-old saga that was Mao Zedong's favorite. Then the outlaws and outcasts build Sanctuary; Canudos is a community with no property, no money, no taxes, no hunger, and no marriage. The government of Brazil surrounds Canudos and blows it up. Vargas Llosa foretells this destruction from the beginning, explosions and prophecies flashing backward and forward in time. The global novelist of the future has to imagine the commune winning so that there will be no war and no end of the world.

I have never tried writing a novel by looking at it as a whole first. I've never before given away the ending and the effects — how I want readers to react. Ideas for a global novel are rushing in to fill some empty sets that have been tantalizing me for a long time. William Burroughs said, "There's no such thing as a great Buddhist novel." Akira Kurosawa tried making a great Buddhist movie, *Kagemusha,* which is about sitting still as war strategy. Pauline Kael said that even Kurosawa can't make a good movie about not moving.

Once upon a time China had three Books of Peace. Those books were hidden and never found, or they were burned, their writers killed, their reciters' tongues cut out. But we can retrieve the Books of Peace by envisioning what could be in them — something like the intimations that I've written here. Should I not have the ability or the years, this which you're reading may have to be it — a minimalist global novel — short enough so the speedy reader can finish up using his or her own words and deeds.

The Last of the Avant-Garde

WILLIAM H. GASS, *Washington University, St. Louis*

A silk doublet to the man who first sights land.

As much as over limitless ocean, the crews of Columbus' three caravels had sailed for a month on such promises. Here, from the commander himself, was the hope of a bright bit of fashionable attire to flaunt, in addition to the annuity of ten thousand copper coins the Crown had offered to the eye that would spy the Indies, to the voice that would cry out *tierra!* like a trumpet. Four hours before their actual landfall, Columbus believed he saw a light, like a curl of foam from the following wind which had driven his fleet all day, and this will-o'-the-wisp was sufficient to substantiate his claim to the reward, although it was a lookout on the *Pinta* who first saw a smear of white beach, or chin of cliff, on the island Columbus would call San Salvador, shouting *tierra! tierra!* then, as if the second shout made his announcement more sincere. One hopes he got the doublet he deserved.

The natives were nakedly naive, and could scarcely have supposed that a few planted banners or embellished sticks were magical symbols meant to confiscate their country, control their souls, and enslave them. They marveled at the ceremony of the landing, which painters have since so faithfully misrepresented, and were pleased by gifts of red caps and glass beads, given to those attending the rites like beer mugs at the ballpark. They were pleased but not possessive, since property did not seem to have a hold on their hearts. This — their generosity — was among the more immediate observations the Spanish made when the Indians freely offered them colorful skeins of spun cotton, raucous parrots, brown clay pots, and jewelry made of shells. In return, they were permitted to play with their conquerors' swords, cutting themselves in their ignorance of Spanish steel. The spectacle must have been amusing.

So the Taino people seemed simple, without guile or the menace of weapons, and trusted the sight of their bodies to any eye. When accounts of their character reached Europe, the story of the noble savage would commence its career in imperial courts. Visions of an actual Eden would inflame many a degenerate imagination, driving more than one mind to utopian extremes.

Even as the foreigners responded with smiles and friendly gestures to the welcome and wonderment of these apparently childlike people, they were sizing up the natives. Within days of the "Discovery," Columbus wrote of the inhabitants: "With fifty men they could all be subjugated and made to do whatever one wished." Beyond the exchange of trifles, mimicry and gesture were the chief means of communication. The fleet's translator was an Arab (no more useful away from Africa than a staved-in barrel), because Columbus had expected to encounter kinky-haired black people, not brown men with hair coarse as a horse's tail, and had brought, in consequence, the kind of trinket the Portuguese had found traded best on that continent: glass beads, brass rings, red caps, and the small round bronze bell used in falconry.

These men who came — with their swords, sails, and cannon — out of the sea: what principally did they desire when they waved their arms and pointed, when they did their dance? Where was their curiosity placed? What did they want to know? What would give them peace?

They had brought their God, more pitiless than death, for Hell was everlasting. They had brought the sway of distant sovereigns, more whimsically tyrannical than the local typhoons. But mainly they had brought their obsession, since they each wanted to know about gold, about bracelets and earrings and any shining object. A country they called Cipangu must lie nearby like a gleaming shoal of silver, an island of spices — this Japan — a reef of gold. A book by Marco Polo had inflamed them. There it was written that palaces roofed with yellow metal existed, where the rain grew savory as soup merely by cascading across such royal covers, in comparison to the common lead which sealed their own back home, and the water which slid, gray as the gray air, over the slates. The floors of these palaces were paved with gold plates two fingers thick. The walls were decorated with richly worked designs inlaid with pearls and other precious stones in numbers, cut, and worth beyond immediate calculation.

The leaders of the expedition were eager to be off. On the next island, perhaps, the ears of its occupants would drip gems, and after that the treasured land itself might light up the horizon — a sighting which could reduce a simple silk doublet to a small wad of moldy rags. So, in addition to the cross of God the natives would be hung on, and the sword of State which would smite them, each member of the ships' company would carry to shore the disease of their greed. Put plainly, they had one motive, and it was money.

The Tainos called their island Iguana, after its most impressive denizen. No spiny lizards live there now, however, and the Tainos themselves are completely extinct — "wiped out," as we say, borrowing what would become a bathroom image.

If Columbus had lied about the sighting of the New World, he was also wrong about where he was. He would sail from cove to cove hoping to encounter Japan, and, failing that, expecting to strike the shores of China farther on. His voyage had made the world seem wider than it had been, but it was not yet believed to be as wide as it was. If the ends of the earth were farther apart than before, the distance was suddenly traversable. In enlarging the globe, Columbus had significantly diminished its scope. The process is familiar, for it continues to shrink in the same way today, so that — symbolically — everybody lives now with their cheek by everybody's jowl. Cultural collisions are as rapid and frequent as caroms in pinball, but they are short shots which — far from producing a Big Bang — go ding, or, sometimes, ding-a-ding, or, sometimes, ding-a-ling.

The Spanish made another error. They believed the natives were naked, as Nature made them, their uncultivated minds ready for religion's roots, their docile spirit perfect for the soul of the servant. Peter Martyr, denying Thomas Hobbes ahead of time, wrote: "They seeme to lyue in that goulden worlde of the whiche owlde wryters speake so much: wherin men lyued simplye and innocentlye without inforcement of lawes, without quarrellinge Iudges and libelles, contente onely to satisfie nature, without further vexation for knowelege of thinges to come." Had nature, then, flattened Tainos' foreheads, deforming their skulls? Had nature clothed them in colors, since some seemed painted black as coal soot or white as oyster shell, while others wore red or displayed a marvelous miscellany? And were a few born with paint all over their bodies, wherever there was skin, or just about the eyes, the face, the nose alone? And had nature spun their cloth or adorned their pottery with grotesque heads, and found them huts of palm thatch to live in? They presented a blank page to the Spanish, as if asking to receive a sheet of writing, but where the dark European word spell fell over them, there was already a cultural message, invisible to the invaders, as if it had been written in the juice of a lemon and blown dry by an unhurried breath.

When Columbus unconscionably collected a few native specimens to astonish his sovereigns, a spirillum was brought home in the bloodstream of at least one exhibit which would infect the venturesome whores of Barcelona, and soon the whole of Europe.

No. The Tainos were civilized to a fault. They baked bread, fornicated standing up, and compressed skulls. Perhaps the Siboney people, whom the Tainos had overcome generations earlier when they migrated to these islands from the mainland of South America, were the original, undeformed, Caribans — the animals of an unspoiled land.

Columbus reached the coast of Cuba on October 28. His small boats scraped onto beaches covered with mangrove trees and backed by mountains, but there were no Japanese to greet him, and no cities made of precious metal to marvel at before reducing them to plunder. He found only a few huts and nets, harpoons and hooks made of bone, as well as some dogs that grunted instead of barking as the species should, and, not kept as pets, useless for alarm, were regularly roasted and eaten like the hogs they resembled.

If there are no Japanese, this must be a little length of the long coast of China. If there are no Chinese, this land must be a bit of India itself, more than merely East. If there are no Indians, these shores must circumnavigate that original oasis, Paradise itself, allowed, perhaps, to grow on alone after Adam and Eve, God and His angels, had abandoned it, its original gates covered with vines and moss somewhere, its great trees tangled, its poetry progressively prose.

Columbus' motives are base, his plans misguided, actions ambiguous, results misconstrued; yet this may be the usual pattern of discovery, whether exploratory or creative, whether we want to claim a country, write the world down, or paint its face. The population of Cuba today, as if history had rearranged itself in order to correct his misapprehensions, is one part Spanish and two parts the Spaniard's expectations; for there are Africans everywhere (although the Arab translator will still be of little use), and Chinese to meet us when we land (despite the fact that neither country has drifted any closer through the passing years and intervening seas). Thus the cultures of three continents have combined on an island which belongs to the general geography of yet another. It's where bloods mix too, with intersecting genes and intercepted feelings, layers of language and an intertwining of signs, acts and aims and meanings whose collision, contradiction, and cancellation — whose modifications, deflections, and comminglings — congeal into the senseless surface of human history — into a crust of pus — just as, against the beaches of the Caribbean, the waves of misery beat without apology or point or remission, as if they were Columbus come to serve up one more culture as the roast dog for another.

We have been traveling in the envelope of an image, pretending to be Columbus, the discoverer of Cathay, pretending to be a naked savage, although our breasts are painted and there is a swatch of cotton cloth over our drizzle parts, and although no man is naked who has a smoking cigar stuck in one hole of his nose. Having inhaled, we hand the rolled leaf to another nostril. The use of tobacco would soon be as prevalent in Europe as syphilis was epidemic, and its importation more valuable than gold.

What is the lesson of this stretch of text called "the landing of Columbus"? The lesson is: we know not what we do, or what we have managed to mean, or what we really value, or in what way, or for whom things will turn out badly. Tobacco (like marijuana, often called gold) will eventually kill more immoderate and unlucky human beings than VD. The lesson is: the motorcar is the scourge of the world, worse than war, worse than the Bomb, worse than any disease. Peanuts, taken captive in Bolivia by the Spanish and resettled in Africa as a source of cooking oil and cattle food in the sixteenth century, are pounded into a soft paste for the palates and purses of impoverished old people in the nineteenth, only to become a favorite with despoiled TV children in the twentieth, lend their name to a figure in a comic strip, and cause cancer in laboratory mice. The lesson is: things are usually what they seem (the natives were naked), yet they are also quite often not what they seem (because the natives weren't naked; they were painted, sported bangles, spoke certain ritual words, left their pubic hair unshaven).

Things are constantly undergoing ontological transformations like characters in Kafka. It looks as though you can't anoint yourself with the same essence twice. In other words: things seem the way they seem because they are what they are; but what they are is not only not what they frequently seem; but what they are is not what they are going to be for very long; indeed, what they are will be some other something soon enough, with new semblances which no longer misdirect us in the same way they once did, from seem to seem and back again, like tock to tick in the standard clock, or loop de loo in the old song, or heigh-di-ho in the new. To explain: although there are lovely allegations to the contrary, Columbus was Italian, born in Genoa, where no one spoke Italian, but a dialect of their own contriving; however, since it was a language no one wrote in, Columbus naturally did not write in it, writing instead in a Spanish full of quaint Portuguese spellings. He did not have to discover the New World. He already was the World to Come.

To explain: I have several uncles — one who dresses like a woman in order to pick up girls, another who occasionally puts on a body stocking very faithfully imprinted with his own body parts put together from a photo, another who sits in cafes in such a way he could be mistaken for an especially notorious dyke, and a friend who arranges words on a page with a look of such meticulousness it is tempting to attribute them to Marianne Moore. That is the lesson.

This view of literature and art and history (and most everything else on a long list) is by no means to be understood as subscribing to the currently convenient suggestion of the modern-day sophists that you can have things the way you want them, because the opposite is the case, you can never have things the way you want them, and what is true stays true, namely, that the natives were naked, that the natives were painted, that they didn't wear beards or shoes; because my uncle had to look like a man in order — you see — to *look* like one; but he had to wear that look in such a way one knew he was a woman who was dressed up very expertly like a man, a woman well-known throughout the city as Demoiselle, the downtown dyke (Orlando in a previous life; Cobra, sometimes, in our present one), each nuance of the masquerade created so as to give the game away in precisely the right manner, at precisely the right moment, for precisely the right reasons, achieving precisely the right effect; for if my uncle passes perfectly as a man, when he is a man already, where is the art? And how is it to be appreciated? Because a powerful prose never fools around but goes straight for the center of life like one of those darts on valentine designs which never flies its page yet breaks apart some sentimental plump red heart like a piece of pitted fruit, and in the puddle of its accumulated *p*s looks back with pleasure upon the improprieties which make it truthful, like a face which has removed its rouge so as to demonstrate the artificiality of innocence. Columbus' boats scrape ashore in Paradise, where Lezama Lima lies waiting.

What is the right effect? After all, someone will be appointed to ask that: what, they are going to wonder, is the effect that should follow from such a list of precisions, from such pretensions in a dollar watch to tell exact times? It is to produce the surprise and shame and exhilaration of a complex desire — in men for a man-made woman maybe (didn't Flaubert say *c'est moi* of Madame Bovary, and James Joyce dress his voice in lingerie at last to bring off *Ulysses*?). The effect? A feel for nuance — the touch like that of a hairy thigh on some spot long neglected, a flicker in a fine actor's face, unexpected, a warm kiss from a stone mouth. The effect? An admission that detail is dominant where quality is concerned, and for any understanding that goes deeper than a dish. For example, the fact that the natives were naked, were painted, wore nothing in one case but a nose plug, that the dogs merely grunted, that there is a Third World rhythm in a certain phrase. The effect? From relations between clothed and uncovered, gold nose plug and bone, the look of the island and its future as a line on a map, from the clear ring of the falconry bell against the long dark sound of the surf, a gleeful squeal at the sight of a gleaming bead, palm shadows under water, from the smell of fish in the bilges of native boats (for had the natives not been naked, they would not have been so immediately seen — living like animals in their homegrown pelts — as likely slaves), from such connections a new order can be formed, a fresh compound with novel emergent properties. The effect, then, in sum? The revelation of a reality which exceeds the philosophers' thin lists, a reality which includes all the banned shades of Being: adverbs, smudges, fudges, malingering and retraction, errors, imbecilities, accidental properties, distortions, simulations, reflections, doubles, nicks and scratches, beliefs so oddly bald that even a wig will slide off easily (isn't it true that without a shadow you cannot claim to have a soul? that lacking its figments a thought would never strike a light? that tarnish darkens and helps define a silverware's design? mold improves some cheese? use most shoes? and that no one is called wise without wrinkles, scarifications, and lines of worry across their face?), hence a reality which does not play down, upend, or undercut one of its constituents on behalf of another (that Columbus wasn't gifted and coura-geous because he was cruel and greedy, that the Discovery wasn't significant because it was callously carried out, sordid, grim, and exploitive, or because the Vikings were technically first), since a rainbow needs no inflation, no myth to make it a miracle, it is wonder enough in itself, as is the sparkle of the stars on the surface of a still sea, sometimes seen by Columbus; nor should these evanescences have to suffer disclaimers, discounts, reductions, as if the rainbow were merely a momentary swash of colored water, one's shade nothing but a shadow, one's wound only a scratch.

The natives lived a low-grade life. They didn't wear clothes but ran about like babies, pleased as punch with baubles, little bells. But it has taken us some centuries to cut our wardrobe for the beach back to the bikini, receive all those vitamins from sun and air, endure stares from dirty old eyes, accept offers from model agencies and movie directors, seize opportunities to appear in ads for beer. Now we know, of course, that the sun causes cancer, the salt air and the ultraviolet rays dry the skin and prematurely wrinkle it, making us look not wise but like sozzled old tennis pros; consequently smart people cover up, the dead-fish look becomes desirable, and we diet because eating is dangerous and we want to be able to get into our skinny minis, not skinny because they are skimpy (remember the sun), but because they are tight (and clearly cut off the circulation of blood to the brain).

When I wore my designer tie around my waist at the nude beach, how differently undressed I was from the natives who met the boats of Columbus, and one reason for the difference is that time has multiplied my avenues of action, so that the meaning of my behavior depends as much on choices not made as on choices chosen, and on a context I understand and can count on — on orders obeyed and orders overturned, on expectations realized and expectations defeated, on the no longer fashionable width of my foulard.

We have heard the lookout, in the naive belief that he has just won ten thousand maravedis, cry out *tierra!* but what did the natives shout? Sail ho! in Tainoese? Break out the castanets, here come the Spaniards? Certainly they ran to the beach to see the show: the landing of the aliens at last, their breastplates gleaming, banners aflutter, splashing about in the surf, gesturing at the skies, and sticking long poles into the sand. Perhaps they hoped that for some generous applause they would be thrown a garter or a rose and find a nice prize in their Crackerjacks. Christopher Columbus, admiral of the ocean sea, the alpha of the avant-garde, has just parted the curtain, stepped before the footlights, waded ashore in the New World.

"Show time! *Señoras y señores.* Ladies and gentlemen. And a very good evening to you all, ladies and gentlemen.... Tropicana! the MOST fabulous nightclub in the WORLD ... presents ... its latest show ... where performers of continental fame will take you to all the wonderful world of supernatural beauty of the tropics."

"Come to the cabaret, old chum."

And we did. We wanted to experience pre-innocent nudity, the latest designs in doublets and other false promises. We wanted to learn the language of layering and other semiological geologies.

Welcome to the cinema, kid.

And we see the private eye in out of the cold, hot for certainties in this our life, preparing to make love to the blond he has just met on the stairs. He gives his clothes a negligent toss, gestures which are meant to hide his potency fears. Under the overcoat a jacket conceals a shoulder holster (which he suspends, with studied insouciance, from the knob of a bedpost). It also encloses a vest which brackets a tie which hangs from a shirt which hugs a torn stretch of underwear beneath which there is a St. Christopher medal pressed into some body hair, and trapped there a small fog of cheaply manufactured scent. Why is he taking his belt off, and not yet his soft felt hat? The PI's clothes are items in an order; each piece presents the possibility of its use again when lifted from its heap on the chair, or its earlier place in a closet, and (since most of the duds this impecunious PI puts on are secondhand) from its once-upon-a-time life on the back of a better bankroll. He shuffles out of his pants and leaves them in a puddle. Not yet the soft hat, the shoes. The overcoat tells us it's winter, the jacket that he's been to a modestly upscale society affair, the holster that he has potency problems, the vest that the movie is set in the thirties, the tie that its owner probably puts his feet in unpolished pointy yellow shoes, while the soiled shirt suggests his socks have holes. The Elvis image on his underwear provides a surprise — gives pause — the tear is pure Marlon Brando — but not the medal pressed in body hair, because we've seen this actor's chest bared before, when he played Pebbles, the bantamweight boxer.

The hair means manly, its gray his age, the medal his terror of trains and other traveling, the scent a memory best left to Marcel Proust, while the entire scene is a routine reenactment of a conventional bumpydump in the stale tough-guy genre, a formula so worn out even its spoofs are old hat like the old hat our PI is still wearing while he rides his blond into the mattress. With his manhood restored by her submissive ministrations (she must have a more important part than I thought), he can fire his gun again, and shoot the villain in the culminating scene so the bad guy catsups broadly before falling from a bridge, through a high window, onto the tracks, and crashing his car which plunges into a river or over a cliff, runs through a store window, careens into the middle of a military convoy, and bursts into flames. Errol Flynn never took off his shoes. You never know when you may want to leave the set in a hurry.

We have been sailing in the holds of three connected similitudes whose names can be recalled from school-kid days in school-kid ways: in *Niña*, the metaphor we might memorize as "Miss Direction" or "Miss Conception"; then, in *Pinta*, the figure we could letter on our fingernails and label like a rock group "CultCrash" (of which more in a moment); and finally, in *Santa Maria*, the vessel which leads and commands the others, whose mast flies an imaginary flag which bears the phrase "the vellum palimpsest," spray-painted on a field of conquistador graffiti.

The *Niña* carries a cargo of confusion, misinterpretations created by false hopes and overweening greed, of deviousness and deformation and misdirection, the unpredictability of distant consequences, routes plotted against the wrong stars which nevertheless steer us straight to immortality. The *Pinta*, for its part, is laden with outmoded habits and pat slogans and flea-infested dogmas, customs and values, and turns of phrase. Its superstitions are more deadly than any disease borne by the trinity it worships: spiritual salvation, secular power, and material wealth. Nowadays, the *Pinta* is the flagship of pidgin culture, hereinafter to be explained. The *Santa Maria* contains the texts which make an absent world real, the arguments which convert lust into reason, profit into exploration, the apologies which will make rape and pillage a virtue, slavery a necessity, extermination expedient. Every error borne to the New World by the *Niña* is written down as gospel on the *Santa Maria;* each custom carried by the *Pinta* is reenacted in congratulatory language on the leader's ship, and constantly corrected too — expanded, amalgamated, revised, erased — till it is crammed like the hold with thefts and borrowings, denials and rejections, one within another like a weevil in a biscuit. The strangers bore arms and trinkets, symbols, Bibles, rosaries ashore. How were the natives to know that they possessed something valuable in the unsaved condition of their souls, or that those small black books were bombs to blow apart the spirit? How were they to know? The natives were naked.

Columbus' day was the dawn of the death of God. The State would shoulder the Church aside in its struggle for power, and the control of culture would pass (by degrees, of course) to the Court. Philosophers began to appeal to Nature and the light of Reason to reorder the chaos into which reality had fallen, and Mammon, the new enemy, emerged from his cave and put on whatever respectability he was able to buy.

Our day is never yesterday; it is always tomorrow; and we have become accustomed to the death of God only to witness, in addition, the death and disappearance of Nature. Power has passed (again, only principally, and by degrees) into Mammon's bank account. The commercial world is the world that's real; economics is the only sound study of value; technology creates the media which control demand and then makes the supplies which will satisfy it. Money is no longer merely a means. It is badge, banner, and holy belief. Philosophers have cast aside a used-up Nature — a mother whose morals proved looser than your average harlot's — and doused Reason, a weak light anyway, and one which persisted in recommending the right way rather than the way one's wants wanted. The world of ideas has become a department store, and democracy (with its toleration of difference, its flattery of the markets) is simply considered the ideology presently best for business.

Meanwhile, we in the West still look East, where we see a billion uncapitalized Chinese, customers without TVs, motorcars, laundry soap, jeans, amplified guitars. And nowadays we can each be, as Saul Bellow said of Augie March, a Columbus of the close at hand, since everything is within easy reach: India, China, Africa, the Middle East, the Indies, Korea, Taiwan, Singapore, Hong Kong, Japan. Entrepreneurs set forth every hour hunting for cheap labor, raw materials, vast markets, big dough. In Columbus' day, culture accompanied Church and State on their enterprises and was forced upon their victims like further chains. But for us, culture is a commodity, values are on the stroll, ideals are tailored to a way of life like hemlines and cuffs, and a culture conquers by being sold.

Literature is less immediately affected by this commercial ebb and flow, because even schlock is confined to its language; the sleaziest porn remains resolutely conceptual and requires a modicum of intelligence to achieve its lubricious results; whereas cooking, comic books, and clothing, cosmetics and the cinema, pictures and paintings, gadgets and cars, merchandise of all kinds can travel from one dunce to another without ever entering the precincts of the mind.

Let's take a trip or two and get a sense of the situation.

A young man in a modified tuxedo carries our suitcase down a narrow door-lined hall. Although the bag is swollen and heavy, he lifts it easily and seems to sail silently along — a silence which should not surprise us, since his feet are bare. Our room has everything: desk, lamps, chairs, veranda, bed, minibar, bath, bureau, closet, phone, oversize TV.

The furniture features blond wood pretending to be bamboo. The television screen will remain gray for the duration of our visit, however, because, except for consular towers which can pick up Australian transmissions, there is no broadcast signal to be received in Papua New Guinea.

A few weeks later we shall sit on the earthen floor of a hut in the middle of a Manila barrio and drink tea from a chipped cup. In front of us, like a shrine, is another blank screen, this one surmounted by a paint can crammed with a miscellaneous gathering of plastic flowers: blooms of wildly different shapes and colors, stems of widely various lengths. The slum is awash with muddy water from recent rains. A communal spigot brings in fresh — we are drinking it — but there is no electricity for the set. There's never been any.

In Papua, again, we see Stone Age men squatting alongside the road drinking soda pop and eating Twinkies. Up in the hills, and at the behest of their elders, high school students are demonstrating tribal dances before an audience of sunburned Aussies and paler English. The students have learned the dances in order to preserve their heritage, and perform them to celebrate their graduation. Spears are thrust with grunts into the side of the sky. The mud man, who lifts his chalky leg repeatedly in the required scatological gesture, wears a wide round watch with a brazenly pink dial. Observant women comment on the costumes and admire the disciplined ranks of the dancers. After the ceremony, the kids skedaddle, piggybacking on motorbikes down the mountain.

Dynasty Hao is a restaurant which has recently opened in Tokyo. Its interior has been designed to resemble a bare-beamed SoHo loft, and its sound system speaks riffy American jazz. The food, however, is spicy Taiwanese: pork dumplings, sauteed pumpkin with garlic, minced chicken in lettuce. The restaurant is the second of this name to be opened by Kiddieland, an upscale Japanese toy store. To find most places in Tokyo requires elaborate directions because locations aren't numbered — there are no addresses — but we can readily get our bearings from the Famous Amos cookie shop nearby, and the Mexican restaurant, La Jolla, which is just across the street. Young mothers naturally frequent Dynasty Hao after purchasing Cabbage Patch dolls and buying Babar books. I'm told that their favorite drink is Perrier flavored with a Japanese plum brandy. The liquor list spells it "Perie" but Perrier is what it is. Misspellings are part of the fun. So is incomprehensibility. A place in Nagoya calls itself Café L'emoi. Can we figure out whether the sign is trying to advertise the "Me Café," or whether the place really intends to call itself "Café Flutter" — better yet, "Café Anxiety"? Perhaps, to the Japanese, the sign only says "French."

On the other hand, we might prefer to visit the authentic twenties speakeasy where entertainments put on during that roaring time have been precisely duplicated: ambiance, menu, and music recreated to delight the senses of another country and another age as if that twenties way of life had spread instead of waned, as if that allegedly rollicking era had never passed.

Minced pigeon is a popular dish in many of Tokyo's Chinese restaurants, although the bird is sometimes surreptitiously replaced by chicken. However, if your food is Taiwanese, your surroundings American, your management Japanese, your owner a toy store with a California-style name, then it scarcely matters what has been minced and hidden in the hay: what you are eating is pidgin.

A tribal mask is made after an old pattern. The medicine man once wore it to frighten snake venom from a bite. The mask is purchased by a poet who christens it Omoo, after Herman Melville's novel, hangs it on the wall of his study, and calls it his muse. The poet's poetry may be pure Iowa City, but his inspiration is pidgin.

I intend to give Phyllis, for her birthday, a museum's replica of a necklace found on an Egyptian archeological dig. We shall eat in an Italian restaurant, see a French movie based on a Russian novel, attempt to make love Amerindian style on a futon covered by an old-fashioned patchwork quilt of Shaker design. We are living pidgin. Why not? A pidgin culture is no doubt the culture of the future.

I call it pidgin in honor of all those wonderfully twisted tongues which were the consequence of an often abrupt collision between cultures — initially the speech of sailors, stevedores, servants, whores, missionaries, merchants, and later of anyone else who wanted to pick up some loose change from the wreck. Pidgin is a subordinate and fotch-on lingo almost entirely commercial in origin and aim. It begins as a loose mix of two or more languages with the most dominant partner pidginized, or reduced to speakability, by the presumably weaker one (the pidginator, I suppose); hence those colorful, indicative names: Tourist Turkish, Sandalwood English, Chinook Jargon, Plantation Pidgin, Miskito Coast Creole, Pitcairnese, Beach-la-Mer, Ngatik Men's Language, Sango, Taki-Taki, Town Bembo, and the like. The result seems (deceptively) like shanty or shack talk, oral in origin, built of whatever is handy and floating along in the speech stream, often of similar sounds if not similar senses. Drastically simplified in both vocabulary and syntax, pidgin omits articles and pronouns, other niceties; it relies on one verb form, usually the infinitive; and it is frequently accompanied by vowel doubling and other reiterative verbal gestures, generally for the sake of imitation and emphasis.

Pidgin becomes what is called creole when, after several generations, there exist speakers for whom it is a first language. We are mostly in a pidgin culture phase, but we shall see a creole culture soon, when the children of popcult parents will be born as full of fizz as the bottle is.

Pidgin only slowly reaches written form, and phonetic spelling further distorts what we see, so that sentences which might make reasonable sense to even an untutored ear will seem incomprehensible to the eye. If we know that in Melanesian Tok Pisin, the wallaby is called a *sikau*, then only a whiff of Portuguese (*pinis save* — possess knowledge) may throw the ear off the scent:

> Long taim i go pinis ol sikau i no save kalap kalap olsem yumi lukim nau. Ol sikau i ron nabout olsem dok.

> [A long time ago wallabies did not know how to hop. They got about as dogs do.]

Pidgin culture, on the other hand, is as visual as these languages are oral, and it misleads the eye as "olsem Tok Pisin" does the ear. Such cultures are secondary overlays of an original, of course, and whereas they reveal the presence of a desire, they conceal its customary body. Pidgin culture is commercial — to repeat the point — as unstable as its markets, rootless (at first), simplified, crude, repetitive, blunt. Apart from its business use, this is pidgin culture's considerable appeal: its icons have no history; they belong to a more exciting, shameless Now; they can be appreciated and adapted with ease, abandoned without qualms; and to teenagers, pidgin culture seems about as old as they are. Neither knows yet how to *kalap kalap*.

It is to the teeming cities of Japan we must turn if we want to experience pidgin culture in its purest manifestation. Gertrude Stein once said, with her customary shrewdness, that the United States was the oldest country in the world because it had been in the twentieth century longest. Now the *olsem* sort of thing, concerning the next century, can be said of the Japanese, who are the leaders in culturally what is to come: the multitudinous and fizzling finale of the avant-garde.

If we take a walk in Tokyo, we move like an eye through the polyglot jive of a contemporary sentence, one which we might have met before in a novel like Severo Sarduy's *Cobra*, a work which resembles this newly arrived world so completely we cannot locate the likeness; our fingers find the seam between them, which we believe should feel like a scar. It is the world of the changeling, of cultural theft and simulation, the stray's turf, the mongrel's yard, a world where the entire population of one country may be exiles from another, a world which speaks pidgin, knows only fragments from trivial texts — surfaces, gestures, moments — a compaction of images, a world where a walk is a new way of reading.

And what walks they are! Amid the clatter of construction, through the purposeful crowds of people, past an apparently limitless variety of shops, their small windows crammed with color and charm and enticing wares, the stroller gravely proceeds, accompanied always by a wild webbing of wires overhead, by signs pasted on walls and windows, strung like banners, hung like flags, mounted like pictures, billboarded and postered and sprayed, outlined in gaudy lights, cut like cookies into odd, catchy, or amusing shapes (that of the lobster, crab, dragon, robot, rocket, shooting star), and preceded by others fastened to the edges of facades like tear-off tabs, since Japanese streets enter buildings, which are often arcades in any case, to rise with the elevators from floor to floor (dress shop on three, disco on seven, noodles on nine), because it is believed that customers will want to know, while still outside, making their approach, what earthly delights each level will deliver. There are signs which cover the entire side of a structure like a sandwich board, or signs which box in the water tank on the roof or fall in the form of a full skirt down the front of a store. These signs do not preen like the nighttime daydream neons in Las Vegas; they are busy as brokers on the floor of the bourse, jostling one another, competing for attention, crying out, waving, hooting and whistling, begging, cajoling, promising, threatening, hollering in every script and kind of character, diction, and design, until to the din of the ear is added the scream-rate of the street; all this noise for the eye, and a vaporous distillment of what seems to be every human urgency, energy, and need (as well as so much which is meaningless, so much which is mean) begins to rise in a steamy cloud the way rain does from hot pavements; and the pedestrian's spirit, in this manner assailed, responds in spite of itself: desires diversify, plans expand, and a sense of a generously enlarging life fills the scene as far as the eye can catch sight of a sign and decipher its signal.

When the Germans came to the United States, they brought their sauerkraut, their beer, their Bach, and the Irish brought the fistfight, and the Italians tomato sauce and tenors, and now the Mexicans have smuggled chocolate chicken and big hats across the border along with themselves; but bits of foreign culture arrive in Japan without the foreigners or any inhabitants who might represent the practice, only technicians sometimes, whose business it is to see that the look of things is right. Tok Pisin is invented so that commerce can proceed; pidgin culture, on the contrary, comprises the very goods in question, the articles in trade. What is purchased is a fragment from another way of life, a simulacrum, a living image. Even Japanese sociologists have been puzzled by the popularity of places like Disney World, a replication now complete on recovered land in Tokyo Bay and a huge hit with Japanese of every age and station. Authenticity is an obsession. For a time, the staff was instructed to "act American," and was consequently trained to glad-hand, wave, and grin, at everyone and in every direction. Yet what can "authentic" mean in the Kingdom of Kitsch? And what do the Japanese make of these Western fairy tale and popcult figures? these castles and keeps? these pirates and Indians?

Omoo, the poet's muse, hangs on a wall in the Midwest, a vaguely powerful presence still, his face composed of cowry shells, his beard made of thornbush, tusks curling out of his nose; but where he hangs, he is required to substitute for Euterpe, a virginal daughter of Zeus, who goes about in a white nightie and strews leaves.

Mickey Mouse and Roger Rabbit make complete and perfect movie stars, because, with them, there is no original; only make-believe is real; and where, like Santa Claus, their image is, they are — that's it. Nor is any photo of Marilyn Monroe more Marilyn than any other — all are equally all there is. It has been frequently remarked how rapidly this media-made reality is overtaking the old. That takeover is nowhere more marked than in the replacement of the traditional Japanese print by the present-day sadomasochistic comic book and the incarceration of Utamaro's floating world within a darkly ruled newsprint frame.

Modern media make it easy. The camera replaces its object with an image; the recording collects a voice as disembodied as an angel's;

words are removed from their authors and given to fictions to speak; fashions in food and dress and feeling are transmitted instantly from Copenhagen to the Congo, from Tashkent to Tokyo; and a new Pakistani restaurant opens, or a boutique that sells baskets from Somalia, while a hot song about world hunger written in Palm Beach hits the charts and makes the rounds.

Written roughly thirty years ago about an experimental novel by Maurice Roche, this remarkably prescient paragraph of Severo Sarduy describes one possible novel of the future:

> a new literature in which language will be present as the space of the *act of encoding*, as a surface of unlimited transformations. Transvestism, the continual metamorphosis of characters, references to other cultures, the mixture of languages, the division of the book in registers (or voices) would all, through their exaltation of the body — dance, gestures, every possible somatic signifier — be the characteristics of that writing. The Carnival, the *Circus* — which is the title of a more recent book by Maurice Roche —, and erotic theater would be the privileged places where fiction could unfold. Beyond censure, beyond common thought, in this scene of writing all former and contemporary texts of the book would converse, all the *translations* that exist within a single language would become explicit. This would be a literature in which all currents, not of thought but of the language that thinks us, would become visible, would confront their textures within the scope of the page. (*Written on a Body*, translated by Carol Maier [New York: Lumen Books, 1989, p. 41])

The fragmentation of the streetscape, the scatter of images, the clutter of cables and connectors, the piecemeal movement of crowds, the wholesale collision of cultural symbols and consequently the frenetic jumble of sense and sensation which is the sum of any city stroll comprise a region of chaos that stands in astonishing contrast to — for example — a cemetery hidden in the center of the Roppongi district, one of the most culturally vibrant sections of Tokyo. Here, just out of the street scene's sight, in a quiet that belongs to the country and where bird song instead of car horn can be heard, ancient monuments in solemn memorial rows create the illusion of yet another city, one of broad avenues and breathing spaces, of a discipline achieved in death, and an arrangement of paths and stones (like the skull that was supposed to sit — memento mori — on the scholar's desk) which one hopes will one day save the ballyhoo surrounding it short blocks away and rejoin the many purposes, presently of no importance, which these tombs belie to something steadfast, significant, and rooted.

There are three different kinds of culture in our midst, competing for our loyalty and their survival. There is the traditional: the allegedly pure and unbroken racial, religious, and geographical oneness of Japan, for example — sacred, tribal, local, inbred, slow (what the Tainos had, for all I know). It keeps its language uncontaminated, as the French do, by employing academic guardians who prevent borrowing and stamp out low use. The techniques of the arts are not simply means, but are pursued with an almost religious devotion, the way rituals are performed, and they are disciplines accordingly taught by sages, masters, adepts, and the materials of the arts (words, wood, ink, tones) receive the reverent attention due a deity. Subjects are few and well worn, themes are metaphysical, and success is judged on the basis of minute and subtle differentiations. Tradition values repetition, refinement, nuance, hierarchy, and customs' practices literally identify and define a people. Originality is not sought and anonymity is gratefully accepted. The culture as a whole deems itself the servant of some greater good and higher truth. Although it speaks piously of the past, it does whatever it can to halt the clock and prevent change, never allowing the past to become past but keeping the past present right on into the future. The timelessness of a certain time is its design. Such cultures are fundamentally defensive, however, and are, in large part, formed by their fear of the foreign.

The New World, whether American, Caribbean, or Canadian, is more of a mongrel. We know it well, this culture of assimilated immigrants, of mixtures and modifications both genetic and historical. These elements, however, are still firmly attached to their original roots, so they can be accurately called transplants. The Chinese restaurant which opens in Toronto may modify its cuisine to suit North American tastes, but it is very likely to be owned, managed, and staffed by a single extended family of Chinese. The culture is radically impure, generously open, and profitably plural. It fears homogeneity (a result implicit in the image of itself as "a melting pot") but what actually occurs is the creation of a kind of stew made of many discernibly different ingredients. Ethnic collisions are constant in such societies; remnants of tribalism (which characterizes the first type of culture on my list) desperately resist assimilation and sometimes seem to stay alive only to nurse resentments and hurt feelings. The conflicts they encourage may cause mongrelized communities to come apart from within.

The contemporary culture of the commercial world is certainly all things to all sorts in all ways and times: hybrid (as well as hyped), vibrant (through vacillating), changing (however aimlessly), plural (if simply numbered); but it works solely with surface because it has no roots and is always being shipped; it avoids fundamental conflicts by refusing commitment; and the kind of "culture" a person has depends upon what he or she can afford, what is presently "the rage," and the image that person wishes to project. "Projection" is a key word. "Lifestyles" (another talismanic term) alter as one's status improves and as income increases. Every product is claimed (and believed) to be uniquely wonderful in its own place and time, so that you dress and drive according to a hierarchy of appropriate pleasures and a subtlely informed level of funding.

Here the rites of spring are spring, the trappings of office are the office, the symbols of power are the power, naturally the medium is the message, so that literally everything can become a possession and be for sale. Shortcuts to Nirvana are universally appreciated, and loyalty lasts as long as the utilities are paid. In pidgin culture, nature is as dead as the dodo. There are, of course, parks and preserves, where pieces of the corpse have been pleasantly packaged. The courthouse disappears as a building type. Instead, playgrounds and ballparks are popular, since any civic sense is expressed by fervently backing the town team. Museums are built to house this culture's sacred objects, valued for artistic qualities only because of the myths which have been made for them (rivaling the traditional tales of the doings of the gods), and really prized for their rarity, their monetary halo, their material presence. These are objects which have "made it."

Lacking cultural definition, selves are consequently bought like stoves. Identities are assumed, parts played, beliefs and passions put on and off like clothes — enacted, dreamed — in a world which is half theater, half movie screen with its fast and funky flick of image.

The three divinities with their dominions (God, King, and Cash — Church, State, and Corporation), the three cultures (Tribal, Mongrel, Pidgin), the three realms of value (the Sacred, the Natural, and the Social), the three sirens and their songs (Priest, Politician, Sophist), the three ships of Columbus (Error, Inertia, Propaganda) crisscross, collide, conflate so as to make a kind of malformed matrix and misguiding map of our confusions — misguiding because to be misguided is the only way to get where we are going when it's nowhere we want. Welcome, stranger, to the Mardi Gras, to FestivoVille, Autoramaland, Whimsey-World, the Moneymall; come to the cabaret.

How easy for Jane Austen to represent the real when it was real; how agreeable for Walt Whitman to celebrate our multiplicities, reduce our differences as if we were all of the same indeterminate sex and sensibility; how odd now the novel seems, however, when Cabrera Infante or Severo Sarduy holds that selfsame mirror up to nature which once, at least, pretended to a clear and single image, or to distortions carefully cataloged and rigorously defined; for the kaleidoscope controls its duplications, propels its parts into pleasantly prefigured regions, and lets us appreciate what symmetry can do; whereas the streets and sentences of our present life run as rampantly unmarked as Tokyo's, the new New World we have landed in, not "new" as Columbus knew it, where the equally ancient are seen with eyes made babylike by strangeness, but "new" as toothpastes and deodorants are: freshly named, differently designed, recampaigned, price slightly raised.

The last of the gods was long ago consumed. The last of the Mohicans became a novel, then a film. The last of the avant-garde is diet.

In an effort to acquaint their children with a heritage they ought to treasure, as the Papuan pupils were taught their tribal dances, Japanese secondary schools send their pupils in uniformed hordes to every notable hill and noble shrine and important museum. It does not matter where you are, by train and bus and cable car, they will arrive in numbers so noisy and innumerable there will be no place on the garden paths, no space in the temple grounds, no silence for a thousand yards, nothing to consider but girls in navy blue sailor suits and boys in paramilitary boy scout uniforms, teeming behind teetery flags and flocking to every souvenir shop, where unfortunately they do not stay. For the serious tourist, they are a fatal plague. It is not that they misbehave. There are simply so many of them that they cannot possibly appreciate even the company of one another. Communities beset by starlings have my sympathy. Kyoto is kids.

And the question is whether such outings will keep the children from speaking anything but fad, but pop, but comic-book-balloonese. The answer is as clear as my FM station where I can catch three minutes of a symphony by Beethoven between shopping mall and fitness center.

These schoolish excursions are pure pidgin (as they are in our country, much of the time); they are jamborees; they are photo opportunities; they are candy consumption conventions; they are pleasantly empty spaces between cracked books. They are postmodern promenades. And the sacred will be strolled from the pathways, just as our abbreviated visits to the classics seem scheduled for days when their fires are out, when the tinkle-twinkle-tingle of the teacher's commentary obscures the fact that every real work of art is subversive (often the more so when it looks tame); that every fine painting they fail to observe, pushing their companions along the wall, every right note they ignore while talking to their neighbor, every mot juste their eyes race over, every beautiful building they trash, is an enemy of all they will be allowed to hold dear: that Kodachrome of their parents in its fake silver frame, the stone bald eagle egg, the poem which begins "My country 'tis of thee," a dance card from prom night, old Beatles records, roach clip, letter sweater, recliner chair; yet there should be no occasion for fear, since art is an impotent enemy, the merest indifference disarms it, its "to be" is indeed "to be perceived"; and what can be thought through the sleep of Reason, and what can be heard in the Land of Loud?

The class will form up for its portrait. Columbus would have described them in his log, choosing his words carefully because they'd be read by the queen, and painters would later embellish their canvases on the basis of his account. Not now. Only the old Old World is verbal. The class will form up for its portrait. Please. Columbus would have kidnapped a few to take back to Spain. A camcorder could have caught expressions on faces delighted by beads. Images do not die in the same way the Indians did: coughing up their food, watching the waves in terror, wasting away. The class will form up for its portrait. Please. All in uniform. Not a one naked. Not a one painted. But every one cute as bees' knees. The photographer will duck under his faded black shroud. In the background, still standing, an ancient shrine under industrial dust. Where once, by pulling on a rope, you could have called the gods. The photographer will duck under his faded black shroud. And wait the smiling moment . . . And wait the solemn moment . . . And wait the sunshiny split-second . . . And wait . . . And wait . . . Nearby, a Japanese tourist will snap the snapper snapping the kids. And a little to the right, a bit above, I shall take the metaglossy, making sure that, with the shiny split second behind me, I shall get my shadow in the shot. It's only right. After all, aren't we all, already, in the picture?

Columbus in the Novel of the Americas: Alejo Carpentier, Abel Posse, and Stephen Marlowe

RAYMOND D. SOUZA, *University of Kansas*

Samuel Eliot Morison, the noted historian and biographer of Christopher Columbus, once complained about the many "Columbian crackpots" whose interpretations of the famous admiral depended more on imagination than rigorous historical investigation (Morison 1974, p. 21).[1] Kirkpatrick Sale in his recent revisionist study of Columbus and his legacy maintains that "there is probably no other area of modern history with more elaborate fantasies pretending to be sober fact than in Columbian studies, even in works by the most celebrated and reputable" (p. 20). Sale counters the view of Columbus as one of the great men of history, fostered by writers such as Washington Irving and Morison, with his own vision of the admiral as a "restless, rootless man" (p. 54) and as a paradigm of forces that have wreaked incalculable damage on the people and environment of the Western Hemisphere.

When one moves from the essential "facts" of Columbus' life to the speculative realm of motivation and competence, the panorama of opinions becomes particularly varied, ranging from Morison's (1974) assessment that Columbus is one "of three of the greatest navigators of history" (p. vii) to those who present him as an incompetent fool who stumbled onto the New World by dumb luck. Since Columbus' four voyages mark the beginnings of a significant European presence in the New World as well as the first steps in the formation of many new nations, it is not surprising that his achievements should generate so much controversy. Arguments about Columbus involve disagreements over origins, a subject that does not lend itself easily to dispassionate

This research was supported by a grant from the University of Kansas General Research Fund.

discourse. When we relate stories about Columbus, we reveal what we believe our civilization has accomplished and who we think we are. Our perception of the present and future is shaped by our conception of the past, and this process is an act of human volition.

The divergent assessments of Columbus bring to mind Hayden White's contention that historians are basically storytellers who prefigure their interpretations, casting a particular story, for example, as a romance, tragedy, comedy, or satire. White (1973, pp. 1–2) points out that a number of "continental European thinkers — from Valery and Heidegger to Sartre, Lévi-Strauss, and Michel Foucault — have cast serious doubts on the value of a specifically 'historical consciousness' " and have "stressed the fictive character of historical reconstructions." According to White, historians also select aesthetic strategies that enhance the particular emplotment they elect to use. In addition to the fourfold categorization of plot, White (1973, pp. 1–42) employs tetradic formulations for style, world view, and ideology. Following a tradition that extends back to Giambattista Vico, White believes that history is a human creation and that we decide what it is and how it is to be told. He argues that a number of aesthetic decisions are made in forming a text that purports to tell what really happened, and that there are more similarities between historical and fictional renderings of the past than one might suppose. Since art is one of the few methods we have for suspending time, it is not surprising that fiction is one of our principal means of coming to terms with history.

White draws from a number of theorists who are concerned with creative expression, and his emphasis on aesthetic factors is germane to literary scholarship. His categorizations of the plotting, stylization, visionary theorizing, and epistemological interpretation of history are appropriate for fictions that use events and figures from the past as major referents. Keeping in mind M. M. Bakhtin's (1981) assertion that "when the novel becomes the dominant genre, epistemology becomes the dominant discipline" (p. 15), this study will concentrate on the epistemological and tropological grounding of the texts under discussion, or what can be termed the grammar of knowledge and perception.[2] Following White's lead, we will consider history a human creation that is articulated in speech and writing. That is, it is linguistic, and therefore a tropological entity (Mellard 1987, p. 86). As Ricardo Pau-Llosa (1988) has explained in an interview, tropes are indicative of the way "the mind organizes perceptions of events and objects. . . . the agency of these tropes in consciousness is what enables us to synthesize sense impressions and turn them into thoughts, memories and ideas. That is, tropes are the software of consciousness. Without them, perception would be a jumble of sense impressions" (p. 18).

Alejo Carpentier's *El arpa y la sombra* (*The Harp and the Shadow*), Abel Posse's *Los perros del paraíso* (*The Dogs of Paradise*), and Stephen Marlowe's *The Memoirs of Christopher Columbus with Stephen Marlowe* provide recent Cuban, Argentine, and North American views of the famous admiral. These are historical fictions, and by this I mean that they are novels in which the relationships between the creative imagination and specific historical referents are more than incidental. Although they are fictional works, they share the interest of historians in the historiography of time and place and are concerned with how entire societies are transformed by change. However, these novels are highly imaginative and enter the realm of the fantastic in their narrations of the unfolding of history. They are, in every sense of the word, narratologically governed accounts of the past in which knowing is intimately linked to telling. That is, they privilege narrative in their attempts to structure, understand, and interpret history.

El arpa y la sombra contains the most unfavorable portrait of Columbus in the three works under discussion, a continuation and development of a preoccupation with the admiral manifested in Carpentier's masterpiece, *El siglo de las luces* (*Explosion in a Cathedral*). *El arpa y la sombra* is cast in a satiric mode, but its most predominant tropological strategy is metonymic. Carpentier's desire to discredit Columbus, Queen Isabella, and some leaders of the Catholic church leads him to emphasize cause-and-effect relationships, but he combines these strategies with an engaging use of satire and synecdochic characterizations that link the admiral to a number of human vices.

Carpentier views the historic forces unleashed by Columbus' discovery as essentially tragic. The encounter between European and Amerindian civilizations in the sixteenth century was devastating to the indigenous populations, to the extent that Tzvetan Todorov has termed it "the greatest genocide in human history" (1984, p. 5). It is difficult for Carpentier to conceive of such evil results not having an unsavory first cause. He pictures the Native Americans who were taken to Europe by Columbus as being dismayed by the civilization they encountered, particularly by the lack of hygiene and the social inequities. In Carpentier's novel, Columbus is not a harbinger of a better social order or morally superior forces.

El arpa y la sombra is centered on an attempt by Pope Pius IX to have Columbus declared a saint by the Catholic church in the nineteenth century. Known as Count Giovanni Maria Mastei-Ferretti before becoming Pope Pius IX, he was the first future pontiff to travel to South America, when he was assigned as auditor to the papal legation in Chile in 1823. In Carpentier's account, it is during his stay in South America that Mastei conceives the idea of the need for a new saint to reaffirm the connections between the Old and New Worlds and to counteract dangerous concepts that are sweeping the globe. Mastei emerges in this novel as a skilled and cunning reactionary, preoccupied with the ideas concerning the separation of Church and State and the reaction against Spain during the wars of independence. Mastei (Pius IX) and Columbus provide links between Europe and the Americas, and the binary structure of the novel is based on these historical referents. In both cases, the link is portrayed as cynical, manipulative, and corrupt.

El arpa y la sombra opens in Rome with Pope Pius IX retiring to his private residence after a session with the dignitaries of the Church. There he considers the papers that will initiate the long and complicated process required for the eventual nomination to sainthood, but he hesitates to sign the document. This motif of a hand holding a pen and suspended in space is repeated several times in the novel and is indicative of moments of pause and doubt in the life of the pope or that of Columbus. In such instances, the exercise of authority is momentarily interrupted. Tropologically, the hesitating hand functions as a synecdoche, because misgivings about the admiral radiate throughout the text as the traditional image of Columbus is subverted. In the semantics of the novel, doubt eventually is displaced by opposition as the conventional view of Columbus is first suspended and then reformed. The trope also functions as a rupture or linking device, allowing the narration to expand into the past, for as the pope pauses to examine the document, he begins to recall his trip to the Americas, and an extended analepsis recounts his travels. In this respect, the trope initiates the hermeneutical process of the novel.

The second of the novel's three major sections opens with an interior monolog by a dying Columbus waiting for the arrival of his confessor. Because this is the most extensive section of the work, one critic has concluded that the novel is essentially a "false biography" in the manner of Robert Graves' *I, Claudius* (Barrientos 1986, p. 45). The narrative patterns of the first section are repeated in the second as a character relives key moments in his life. And just as the pope had reread letters he wrote while in the Americas, Columbus goes through the journal of his first voyage of discovery, deconstructing his own creation. He shamefully observes, for example, that there are only a few mentions of God but hundreds of gold. The reappraisals of historical documents involve the reader in a recasting of history.[3] When Columbus fails, in *El arpa y la sombra*, to find significant quantities of gold, he attempts to initiate a slave trade of Native Americans. Royal displeasure brings that scheme to a halt, so he resorts to the expediency of words, creating the legend of a promised land. Carpentier's Columbus takes advantage of whatever is at hand and moves in metonymical fashion from one substitution to another, from gold to human flesh to words.

Carpentier uses a metaphor of a series of boxes within a box to convey the complex and deceptive personality of Columbus and to suggest the investigative modality of his narration. Carpentier's novel is conceived as the final event in a moral drama in which the true nature of an evil being is revealed and historical justice is served. Carpentier portrays Columbus as a seat-of-the-pants navigator, a liar, and an opportunist. When Columbus recalls his marriage to Doña Felipa Perestrello, he emphasizes her family's connections in the Portuguese court and describes her in terms reminiscent of Juan Ruiz: "además de ser hembra placentera, estaba emparentada con los Braganzas y ésta era puerta abierta — más de una cosa se me abría en este casamiento — para entrar en la corte de Portugal y armar allí mi tinglado de maravillas" (besides being a beddable female, she was related by marriage to the Braganzas and that was an open door — more than one thing opened to me in that marriage — to the Portuguese court where I worked by marvelous deceptions) (Carpentier 1979, p. 83). Carpentier's Columbus also has a sexual relationship with Queen Isabella, operating as a sort of Genoese Don Juan who charms his way to fame, glory, and fortune.

Carpentier casts history as an object of masculine energy — it opens to the guile and probings of a restless Columbus. Such activities and the often repeated trope of a pen suspended in space unmask the hidden motives behind the actions and writings of Pope Pius IX as well as those of Columbus. The pope's effort to associate Columbus with the deity through canonization represents the ultimate appeal to authority,

an attempt to legitimatize all the creations the Columbian enterprise
has fathered and/or authored, but these attempts are rendered impotent
by the judgment of history. When Columbus' spirit dissolves at the end
of the novel after witnessing testimony concerning his possible beatifi-
cation, the full moral authority of the text falls on this historical figure,
delivering a verdict of condemnation. This final judgment is indicative
of the novel's aspiration to redemption from history as well as its
contemplation of the mystery of temporality.[4]

Of the three novels under discussion, Abel Posse's *Los perros del
paraíso* makes the most extensive use of the fantastic, frequently project-
ing characters and events into the realm of the mythological. Winner
of the Rómulo Gallegos International Prize in 1987, Posse's work provides a vast and entertaining panorama of Western history from the reign
of Henry IV of Spain to the end of Columbus' career. *Los perros del paraíso*
also narrates aspects of the pre-Hispanic cultures of the New World and
undermines some commonly held beliefs about them, particularly their
assumed isolation from one another and the rest of the world. Posse
reveals in such surprising linkages his interest in creating an interconnected vision of history.

Posse's work moves from fragmentation to unity for the reader, and
this aesthetic experience is conveyed by the predominance of metaphor
in the novel. Objects are compared to one another with little consideration given to time or space. For example, when Francisco de Bobadilla
is sent to the New World to investigate Columbus' administration of the
colonies (an excursion that would result in Columbus returning to
Europe in chains), one of his captains receives the visitor with a
calculated practicality that is compared with the way Hitler dealt with
Hindenburg many centuries later (p. 249). *Los perros del paraíso* frequently mixes different historiographies; in one passage it is suggested
that the incomprehension that exists between the Incas and the Aztecs
is due to the former being socialistic and the latter capitalistic.

Sometimes such syntheses depend on the insertion of an
astonishing detail. For example, the inhabitants of the New World are
well aware of the existence of other cultures because strange objects such
as rosary beads and condoms are carried from the Old World by ocean
currents. In this episode an eighteenth-century English invention appears on the shores of the Americas three to four centuries before its
creation, a discrepancy the narrator is well aware of, because he mentions the supposed inventor, Lord Condom, to exploit the metonymy,

and describes English lovers throwing prophylactics into the Thames River (p. 34).

Although the key tropological strategy is metaphorical, the novel evidences a wide range of tropes, particularly irony. There is little that escapes the subversive scrutiny of ironical and hilarious humor in this novel. The narrator satirizes the religious ideology of the Spaniards by having an Aztec leader attempt to convince his fellow citizens to accept the foreigners because of the gentle nature of their moral creeds. The ingenuous Aztec believes a new age is dawning because he takes literally the religious doctrine the Europeans profess.

In addition to being a tongue-in-cheek historical account of an era, Posse's novel is a sophisticated parody of historical narrative. Each of the four major sections of the work begins with one of the most basic of historical tools, the chronicle, but highly imaginative and humorous elements are inserted. This device undermines one of the cherished procedures of historical investigation, the organization of events in chronological order. Posse mocks and parodies many of his historical sources as well, a technique that Stephen Marlowe also uses.

In one episode in *Los perros del paraíso*, Columbus has an exuberant sexual encounter in the Canary Islands with the dangerous Beatriz Peraza Bobadilla. Beatriz was one of King Ferdinand's many lovers and was known as being "among the loveliest and cruellest . . . of the women of Castile, whom the King openly admired and Isabella sought to remove" (Fernández-Armesto 1975, p. 108). When Columbus meets her on the island of Gomera, she is depicted as a sort of Circe tempting Odysseus. Her cruelty is vividly manifested by a necklace of clitorides she wears. Columbus overcomes this danger by heroically confronting it, and in the depiction of this episode language embodies carnality.

Many of the tropes in Carpentier's novel are organized around references to an explicit pen or an implicit penis, but in Posse's work both sexes are dynamically active. When a young Isabella first appears in the novel, she leads a group of children into the sleeping chambers of her half brother, Henry IV of Castile. She carries a long reed, which she uses to lift the nightshirt of the sleeping king to expose his impotence. This act of revelation (and eventual usurpation) is Isabella's first claim to the throne of Castile. When Henry IV died in 1474, the succession was contested by Isabella and the king's daughter, Juana. Juana's disputed paternity was exploited by her enemies, who referred to her as "la Beltraneja" in reference to her supposed parentage by her mother's lover (Fernández-Armesto 1975, pp. ix–x). Posse's novel uses this pejorative term and describes Juana as having succeeded in placing spies everywhere by the age of five. The civil war between these two women ended with Isabella's victory in 1479, ten years after her marriage to Ferdinand.

In her first appearance in the novel Isabella is wearing a "baby-doll" and is described as "pecosa, rubia, provocadora" (freckled, blond, provocative) (Posse 1983, p. 14). The presentation of "baby-doll" in English as a quotation in the original Spanish text, and the description of Isabella as frequently standing with her legs slightly apart, with her head thrown back, running her hands through her hair, points to Carroll Baker's provocative performance in Elia Kazan's 1956 film adaptation of a play by Tennessee Williams. In addition to being a model for Posse's version of the young queen, the reference is a good example of a source from popular culture. The association is significant because *Baby Doll* contributed to the demise of restrictive film codes in the 1950s (Halliwell 1965, p. 40). In Posse's work Isabella is linked to the unleashing of forces that would be decisive in the formation of the modern Western world. That is, eroticism is related to the will to power and to transformative energies that paradoxically can create or destroy.

Ferdinand and Isabella practice an uninhibited and joyful erotic relationship during the first years of their marriage and reject the affirmation of death that characterized the Middle Ages. But there is also competition and, with time, disillusionment in their relationship, and their energies are externalized into national causes including the expulsion of the Jews and Moors, the terror of the Spanish Inquisition, and the discovery and colonization of the Americas. Ferdinand is portrayed as a crass materialist and Isabella as a willful dreamer, and out of this relationship is born the first totalitarian system of modern times, which imposed by force of arms and the Inquisition its control over all who came under its power (Geyer 1991, p. 21). In Hegelian fashion, Isabella's idealism and Ferdinand's materialism fuse into the conquest of the Americas.

Isabella becomes intrigued with Columbus because she sees in his search for an ideal state, for an earthly paradise beyond Europe, a reflection of her own vision of Eden. During their first encounter, the queen swirls around him like a ballet dancer and then finally places a foot on the chest of the supine Columbus. Under the overpowering presence of his monarch, Columbus' penis shrivels up like a snail recoiling from danger, but he experiences a "panorgasm." In an engaging intertextual reference, the narrator takes issue with Carpentier's "unreal" version of the relationship between Isabella and Columbus, attributing Carpentier's misinterpretation to misplaced democratic sentiments (Posse 1983, pp. 19–20). For Posse, class distinctions between the queen and Columbus were simply too great to allow the unbridled, erotic relationship Carpentier imagines.

Columbus is depicted in *Los perros del paraíso* as born with an abnormal ability to float and as a "superman" who would change the course of history (p. 70). He never takes off his socks when making love, until the end of the novel, when it is revealed that he has a membrane between the second and third toe of each foot. Such imaginative anecdotes are typical of this outrageously original novel.

Posse fuses Columbus' four voyages into one mythological journey and forms a synthesis to capture the essence of the man. When the admiral believes he has found the original site of paradise in the jungle near the Gulf of Paria on the northern rim of South America, he makes some decrees on human conduct and then falls into a hypnotic sleep in a hammock under what he takes to be the Tree of Life. Like Isabella, he is victimized by his own introverted idealism as well as his megalomaniac tendency to confuse proclamations with reality. Columbus remains oblivious to the madness that is unfolding around him as the Native American populations are decimated by ravenous Europeans.

In this section of the novel, Posse effectively uses his technique of transforming sources into minor characters. An infantryman named Todorov expresses impotent rage when a Mayan woman is fed to the dogs (p. 238), a direct reference to an episode described in Friar Diego de Landa's chronicle *Relación de las cosas de Yucatán*, which both Todorov and Posse quote. In this instance, indignation passes from one text to another, recalling a cruel episode in the slaughterhouse of human history. Another soldier, the German Ulrico Nietz, takes the admiral's vision of paradise a step further when he decides that the primitive Indians of the New World are free of the tyranny of the ultimate authority figure, God. In Nietzschean fashion, he announces the birth of superman and proclaims that human nature must be overcome. But there is no overcoming of base instincts by the Europeans in the New World, and a whirlwind of genocidal destruction descends on the hapless and confused Indians. Posse's Columbus is not the crass villain that

Carpentier presents, but he does set into motion a disastrous period of human history.

It is clear from the very beginning of *The Memoirs of Christopher Columbus with Stephen Marlowe* that the narration will assume a synthesis of two identities and the fusion of two consciousnesses as Columbus and Marlowe tell the admiral's story. Since Marlowe is something of a chameleon who has changed his legal name and used several pseudonyms, he must have been drawn to this historical figure who shares his own wanderlust and a sense of being an outsider (Evory 1983, p. 322). This interplay of selves from the fifteenth and twentieth centuries intrigues the reader as different historiographies merge and separate throughout the course of the novel.

As one would expect in a memoir, the narration is in the first person singular, and the reader encounters in this work a more congenial Columbus, a man of more human scale than the mythological figure in Posse's novel or the cynical scoundrel in Carpentier's work. Marlowe focuses on Columbus as an individual person rather than an abstraction. In his novel Columbus has Spanish, Italian, and Jewish antecedents but never feels he belongs anywhere. Afflicted with permanent wanderlust, he always wants to be somewhere else and admits that "sometimes I was even nostalgic for places I'd never seen" (p. 488). A man of great pride and vanity, he becomes enamored of his many titles, particularly "Admiral of the Ocean Sea," which he repeatedly uses. He often refers to himself as a "legend in his own time" and confesses that "during my Julian decade on the northern rim of the Ocean Sea I was bitten by the glory bug" (p. 80). He also shares his doubts and feelings of guilt, confessing that he was a disaster to colonies and "was the worst thing to happen to Italy until Mussolini" (p. 14). He has an uncanny mind for detail and tends to regard people as objects in the historical field. In one episode, while making love to a woman who will come to represent all that is yearned for but never achieved in his life, Columbus recounts: "She lay back on the stack of Persian carpets. The top one was definitely a Kirman" (p. 288). The episode mirrors in humorous fashion Todorov's (1984) grim observation that "in Columbus's hermeneutics human beings have no particular place" (p. 33).

Satire in *El arpa y la sombra* is directed mainly at Columbus, but in *The Memoirs of Christopher Columbus* an ironic and frequently humorous mode focuses on the world as well as the admiral. Little escapes ironic

scrutiny; it may be the Church depicted as participating in the persecu-
tion of the Jews and the overzealous practice of the Inquisition because
it has no faith in its own faith, or Columbus rationalizing hauling Indians
back with him because they will be rewarded "with a trip to Spain,
baptism, and exposure to the incalculable benefits of fifteenth-century
Spanish culture" (Marlowe 1987, p. 203), or the European conceit that
being a Christian means that one is a rational human being. The ironic
modality of Marlowe's novel cuts across the strands of history, unmasking
the motives of those who claim to have established a more humane and
benevolent order.

The concept of history on which Marlowe's novel is grounded is
revealed in some of the metaliterary segments of the text, which is not
surprising, because this is the most self-conscious narrative of the three
under discussion. Columbus mentions history looking over his shoulder
several times as he writes, and in a statement reminiscent of the views
of Hayden White, he observes that "history flows not into but from the
pen of the historian . . ." (Marlowe 1987, p. 21). He also speaks of the
ironies of history and of it being "mostly a toss of the dice" (p. 1). When
Columbus considers the purpose of history, he points out that Herodotus
of Halicarnassus claimed that its main function was to maintain the
memory of outstanding deeds. Columbus then comments dryly that
contemporary history seems more interested in the perpetuation of
terrible deeds but is no closer to the truth. *The Memoirs of Christopher
Columbus* is epistemologically grounded in a world view in which chance
plays a major role and truth is never final or complete. Reality is
conceived as being too complex to comprehend fully, and the threads of
influence running into and from historical events continually move into
broader and more far-reaching contexts.

This world view is vividly conveyed in the text's transformation of
a particular event in Columbus' life. During his fourth voyage, while
anchored off the Bethlehem River in what is now Panama, Columbus
was alone and feverishly ill on the *Capitana*. When he heard the sounds
of battle on shore between his men and the Guaymi Indians and then
the ensuing silence, he climbed to the highest part of the ship and called
for help. After a time, he fell asleep from exhaustion and heard a voice
that admonished him to have faith. Marlowe has transformed Columbus'
account of this event (Columbus 1969, pp. 184–185) into a dialog
between the admiral and a voice Columbus assumes is that of God.
During the conversation the voice uses an image of a series of Chinese

boxes and confesses wondering at times about the next, bigger box —
that is, the voice conceives of itself as only a link in a great chain of
being, an ironic subversion of the original account. The episode in
Columbus' journal implies that his enterprise is part of a grand design
favored by God as the admiral transforms a metonymical rendering into
a synecdoche of cosmic proportions. That is, his individual ordeal
embodies God's plan for the human race.

Marlowe transforms the event by displacing Columbus' trope with
an ironic metaphor in which God is only another voice in a boundless
universe. This tropological move is significant, for it reveals how
Columbus' synecdochic discourse, which is based on a concept of
totalities, is displaced by the ironic and indeterminate modality of the
contemporary age. Columbus views history as an organic whole, and he
perceives reality in inclusive or part-and-whole terms. That is, objects
and events in the historical field are interpreted as representatives of an
overall design. For him microcosmic and macrocosmic entities share
essential qualities. In this episode the discursive practices of Columbus'
time are undermined by the ironic opposition and the contextual
indeterminacy of the present. This key episode illustrates the predominant tropological and epistemological strategies of the text as well as the
displacement of a modality of integration by one that emphasizes opposition, limitations, and inadequacies.

Unlike Posse's Columbus, who is obsessed with the concept of an
earthly paradise, Marlowe's debunks both the myth of a noble savage
and that of a New World utopia, although he is not above exploiting
these "pop-culture ideas" (Marlowe 1987, p. 202) when it suits his
purpose, just as Carpentier's admiral does. Carpentier uses irony and
satire as weapons to demythologize a detested figure, but these rhetorical
strategies are never harmonized with a world view as they are in
Marlowe's work. Carpentier uses humor to ridicule Columbus rather
than to advance his essentially tragic and causal view of history. Like *El
arpa y la sombra*, Posse's work tends to explain the past through a
modality of causality, but this epistemological strategy is not as rigidly
applied as in Carpentier's novel. In *Los perros del paraíso*, objects frequently are identified and compared to one another without regard to
time or space, or they are subverted by imaginative flights of satire and
irony, strategies that undermine historical explanations based solely on
relations of cause and effect.

All three writers see historical forces as moving toward a final resolution, but Marlowe's work is perhaps the most encouraging in the sense that there is more possibility of a harmonious reconciliation of contending forces, if not in the world at large, at least in the attitudes of individuals. However, Marlowe's Columbus is considerably different from the romantic figure portrayed in North American works of the nineteenth century such as Washington Irving's *A History of the Life and Voyages of Christopher Columbus* (1828) and James Fenimore Cooper's *Mercedes of Castile or the Voyage to Cathay* (1840). Those works were conceived in an age that believed in great men, a view that is undermined by the novels discussed in this study, although Posse's mythic narrative evidences vestiges of that attitude in a culture-related sense. However, all three novels share the conviction that individuals can change history. The realm of dynamic possibilities is most restricted in Carpentier's work.

Posse's Columbus senses that things went wrong in a remote past. He longs to return to Eden to begin anew and would like nothing better than to give the apple back (Posse 1983, p. 131). Carpentier's admiral looks to the future to the extent that he decides that he will only tell his confessor things that can be carved in stone (Carpentier 1979, p. 168). Marlowe's Columbus abandons any hope of locating paradise in the past or future and observes that "the word Utopia is a coinage from the Greek and it means 'no place' " (Marlowe 1987, p. 534). The past casts a longer shadow in the texts of Carpentier and Posse than in that of Marlowe, an indication of the burden of the search for a redemption from history. For Carpentier, Columbus' story is like an ungrammatical sentence that must be rectified. For Posse the sentence is unimaginative and sorely in need of embellishment if it is to convey adequately the significance of Columbus' accomplishments. For Marlowe, it is too long and intricate to be mastered, and the period that marks its termination offers only the illusion of closure.

In all three novels, the ultimate trope is Columbus, although it should be noted that Queen Isabella is given equal importance in Posse's work. Indeed, *Los perros del paraíso* implies that the modern world issued from Isabella.[5] Columbus is portrayed in Carpentier's text as the corrupt first mover in an enormous tragedy, in Posse's novel as an exceptional (superhuman) individual who opened Pandora's box, and in Marlowe's work as the first entrepreneur to use publicity and marketing to further his cause. Marlowe's text suggests that a spirit of adventure is one of Columbus' most enduring legacies, and all three novelists depict Columbus as an exceptional storyteller. In their combination of historicity and narrative, Carpentier, Posse, and Marlowe offer different views of the forces of order and disorder operating in human history, and their novels represent various manifestations of the impulse to moralize events. Columbus' achievements herald the conclusion and the beginning of many stories, and the unfolding of complex historical forces. In their portrayals of Columbus and his era, these novels demonstrate how narrating enables us to locate ourselves in history, and how literature and history share what Paul Ricoeur has termed a common " 'ultimate referent' " (White 1987, p. 175).[6]

NOTES

1. Morison's classic study is *Admiral of the Ocean Sea: A Life of Christopher Columbus*, which bears a title similar to that of a novelized account of Columbus' life by another North American writer, Mary Johnston, whose *Admiral of the Ocean Sea* was published in 1923. Morison's work won a Pulitzer Prize.

2. White used the classic tropes of metaphor, metonymy, synecdoche, and irony in his categorization of style — designations I use in this essay. His epistemological categories (world view) are derived from Pepper and deal with how objects and events are presented in the historical field. Although White's and Pepper's classifications will inform my own analysis, I will not use their specific terminology, electing rather to describe each process in general terms. White associates each trope with a world view because he believes a specific paradigm operates in each combination. For White, metaphor emphasizes similarity, metonymy stresses contiguity and/or causality, synecdoche highlights microcosmic-macrocosmic relationships, and irony accentuates opposition and reveals the limitations of the other tropes.

   Some significant tropological studies have appeared in recent years. Particularly noteworthy are Rice and Schofer's study of tropological strategies in modern French literature and Mellard's analysis of tropes in the American novel. Mellard's book, which relies more on White's *Tropics of Discourse* than *Metahistory*, contains an extensive and insightful discussion of White's theories in the first chapter.

3. Forgues has published a detailed article that concentrates on the distortions of historical sources. An opposite tack is taken by Acosta. In an article completed before the publication of *El arpa y la sombra*, González Echevarría defends Carpentier from those who criticize his use of historical sources by concentrating on the importance of allegory in his works.

   There are formidable problems in dealing with the historical records of Columbus' four voyages. For example, the diary of the first voyage comes to us by way of the transcription of Friar Bartolomé de Las Casas, who used a version copied from the original decades after the voyage. Also, modern editions and translations vary greatly.

A new translation of the diary of the first voyage by Dunn and Kelley is an important contribution to the historical record. This bilingual edition contains extensive notes and a concordance. Sale's study contains thorough and succinct summaries of these issues as well as of the controversies surrounding Columbus.

4. González Echevarría has noted that Carpentier wrote this novel while dying from cancer of the throat. He also comments on Carpentier's merging of his own and Columbus' identities in the novel, an insight with which I agree. This raises the issue of Carpentier's text being a partial evaluation of his own career. In one of life's little ironies, Carpentier is buried in the Christopher Columbus Cemetery in Havana.

5. Interestingly, there have been recent attempts by some within the Catholic church to have Queen Isabella canonized, a move that has produced controversy reminiscent of that which greeted Columbus' nomination. One can only imagine the interest Carpentier would have had in such an enterprise.

6. An excellent overview of the interrelations between narration and historical studies is contained in Chapter 3 ("The Revival of Narrative: Reflections on a New Old History") of Stone. The importance of narrative in a number of fields, including history, is explored by Polkinghorne in *Narrative Knowing and the Human Sciences*. Polkinghorne's title focuses on an important aspect of this concern, because "narrative knowing" points to the epistemological nature of this problem and its linkage to storytelling.

WORKS CITED

Acosta, Leonardo. 1980. "El almirante según Don Alejo." *Casa de las Américas* 21, no. 121: 26–40.

Bakhtin, M. M. 1981. *The Dialogic Imagination*. Ed. Michael Holquist, trans. Caryl Emerson and Michael Holquist. Austin: Texas University Press.

Barrientos, Juan José. 1986. "Colón, personaje novelesco." *Cuadernos Hispanoamericanos* 437: 45–62.

Carpentier, Alejo. 1979. *El arpa y la sombra*. Mexico City: Siglo XXI.

Columbus, Christopher. 1969. *Four Voyages to the New World*. Ed. and trans. R. H. Major. New York: Corinth Books.

Dunn, Oliver, and James E. Kelley, Jr. *The 'Diario' of Christopher Columbus's First Voyage to America 1492–1493*. Norman: University of Oklahoma Press.

Evory, Ann, ed. "Stephen Marlowe." 1983. *Contemporary authors*. New Revision Series vol. 6. Detroit: Gale, pp. 321–322.

Fernández-Armesto, Felipe. 1975. *Ferdinand and Isabella*. London: Weidenfeld and Nicolson.

Forgues, Roland. 1981. "*El arpa y la sombra* de Alejo Carpentier: ¿desmitificación o mixtificación?" *Revista de Crítica Literaria Latinoamericana* 8, no. 4: 87–102.

Geyer, Georgie Anne. 1991. *Guerrilla Prince*. Boston: Little, Brown.

González Echevarría, Roberto. 1986. "Carpentier y Colón: *El arpa y la sombra.*" *Dispositio* 11, no. 28–29: 161–165.

———. 1980. "Historia y alegoría en la narrativa de Carpentier." *Cuadernos Americanos* (México) 39, no. 1: 200–220.

Halliwell, Leslie. 1978. *The Filmgoer's Companion.* New York: Avon.

Johnston, Mary. 1923. *Admiral of the Ocean Sea.* Boston: Little, Brown.

Landa, Fray Diego de. 1959. *Relación de las cosas de Yucatán.* Mexico City: Porrúa.

Marlowe, Stephen. 1987. *The Memoirs of Christopher Columbus with Stephen Marlowe.* New York: Scribner.

Mellard, James M. 1987. *Doing Tropology: Analysis of Narrative Discourse.* Urbana: Illinois University Press.

Morison, Samuel Eliot. 1942. *Admiral of the Ocean Sea: A Life of Christopher Columbus.* Boston: Little, Brown.

———. 1974. *The European Discovery of America: The Southern Voyages 1492–1616.* New York: Oxford University Press.

Pau-Llosa, Ricardo. 1988. "Pau-Llosa: A Poet Profile." *Linden Lane Magazine* 8, no. 1: 18.

Pepper, Stephen C. 1970. *World Hypotheses: A Study in Evidence.* Berkeley: California University Press.

Polkinghorne, Donald E. 1988. *Narrative Knowing and the Human Sciences.* Albany: State University of New York Press.

Posse, Abel. 1983. *Los perros de paraíso.* Barcelona: Argos Vergara.

Rice, Donald, and Peter Schofer. 1983. *Rhetorical Poetics, Theory and Practice of Figural and Symbolic Readings in Modern French Literature.* Madison: Wisconsin University Press.

Sale, Kirkpatrick. 1990. *The Conquest of Paradise: Christopher Columbus and the Columbian Legacy.* New York: Knopf.

Stone, Lawrence. 1987. *The Past and the Present Revisited.* London: Routledge and Kegan Paul.

Todorov, Tzvetan. 1984. *The Conquest of America: The Quest of the Other.* Trans. Richard Howard. New York: Harper & Row.

White, Hayden. 1987. *The Content of the Form: Narrative Discourse and Historical Representation.* Baltimore: Johns Hopkins University Press.

———. 1978. *Tropics of Discourse: Essays in Cultural Criticism.* Baltimore: Johns Hopkins University Press.

———. 1973. *Metahistory: The Historical Imagination in Nineteenth Century Europe.* Baltimore: Johns Hopkins University Press.

The North American Novel at the Quincentennial Moment: Everything Is Permitted

LARRY McCAFFERY, *San Diego State University*

> Nothing is true, everything is permitted.
> — Hasan i-Sabbah (c. 1164)

The quote cited in this epigraph, originally uttered nearly 1,000 years ago, came to the attention of American readers during the 1960s, when it appeared regularly in the obsessive and brilliant novels of William Burroughs. Appearing as it did — frequently in the midst of murder, rape, drug abuse, mutilation, and all other manner of aimless violence, animal (and insect) lust, cultural hypocrisy, and depravity — the phrase was taken by many readers as a kind of ironic justification for the hallucinatory and savagely funny episodes that Burroughs' infernal imagination was calling forth. But for Burroughs, as well as for postmodern American authors generally, the phrase points toward a key feature of American fiction during the past fifteen years: its "open-ended" quality, its refusal to accept the notion that there is a single truth, and its willingness therefore to "permit everything" as a means of presenting and representing the many different and often contradictory "truths" and "falsehoods" that comprise American life. As a result, what we find in the most vital and "realistic" fiction appearing in the United States during the past decade is a varied body of writing that provides a good indication of just how much is "permitted" in postmodern American life and the fiction representing this life — including the particular realm traditionally designated as avant-garde fiction.

THE EVOLUTION OF "AVANT-POP"

Using terms such as "postmodern" and "avant-garde" within this context, of course, immediately raises some complex and ambiguous issues. These issues are in fact so complex and daunting that for now I wish to pass over them with a few remarks about why these terms seem so problematic in 1992. To begin with, although nearly everyone today is familiar with the term "postmodernism," no one seems to agree upon exactly what it is supposed to designate. There have by now been dozens of books published on this topic, all of them seeking to clarify and support their own take on postmodernism; but these discussions have succeeded mainly in muddling the picture even further.[1] And the case of "avant-garde" is just as problematic as that of "postmodernism," largely because events within postmodern culture (however we are using that phrase) have tended to blur the distinction between avant-garde and "mainstream" art. In Western art, the concept of the avant-garde has, until recently, been associated with the notion, developed initially in the nineteenth century, of a group of radical artists working outside the mainstream modes of production and aesthetics. These were the "advance guard" of artists who would create works of such striking unconventionality that they would shock and offend the bourgeois — and therefore liberate them from the cocoon of habituation that dulled their responses to the world around them and imprisoned their minds and bodies.

In the United States the avant-garde (or underground) was considered separate from (indeed, opposed to) mainstream art until the 1960s, when, for economic, historical, and technological reasons, the boundaries between the two began to break down. (For a good overview of this entire process, see Ronald Sukenick's important study, *Down and In: Life in the Underground*.) Suddenly there were figures like Andy Warhol, who represented a radical aesthetic but who was very much "aboveground" in his public visibility and financial success. By the late 1960s works that previously would have been considered avant-garde were now available at local bookstores (novels by Kurt Vonnegut, Jr.; Donald Barthelme; John Barth; Joseph Heller; Jerzy Kosinski; and Thomas Pynchon), record stores (landmark experimental albums by the Velvet Underground, the Beatles, Jim Morrison and The Doors, The Stooges, Bob Dylan), movie theaters (the films of Stanley Kubrick, George Romero, John Cassavetes, and such European counterparts as

Jean-Luc Godard, Federico Fellini, François Truffaut, and Michelangelo
Antonioni), or even at the local art galleries (works by "pop artists" such
as Warhol, Roy Lichtenstein, and many others). Thus "avant-pop" was
born.

This interaction between mainstream and avant-garde art continued throughout the 1970s and 1980s. Indeed, for most critics of postmodernism, this blurring of the traditional distinctions between "high"
and pop art has become a central, defining feature of postmodernism
itself.[2] Today such distinctions are, if anything, even more difficult to
maintain. Should rock videos by Madonna, Peter Gabriel, or Laurie
Anderson be considered mainstream simply because they are enor-
mously popular — even though they employ visual and poetic techniques that twenty-five years ago would have certainly been considered
highly experimental? Is William Gibson's "cyberpunk" novel, *Neuromancer*, avant-garde because it employs unusual formal techniques (the
use of collage, cut-ups, appropriation of other texts, the introduction of
bizarre new vocabularies and metaphors)? Or does its publication by the
genre science fiction industry establish it as pop? Were television shows
like "Max Headroom," the early "Saturday Night Live," or David Lynch's
"Twin Peaks" series underground works because they utilized so many
features associated with postmodern innovation — or were they pop art
because they were "merely" television shows?

One of the elements that has made such questions and distinctions
increasingly meaningless is the rise of the "media culture" in the United
States and changes in the way art is bought and sold. Specifically, as
capitalism expanded its operations into previously untapped areas (for
example, the prodigious expansion of the marketing of culture or media
"products"), it began to recognize and then take advantage of a key
practical feature of the free enterprise market system — namely, that
there is a significant and potentially profitable audience for even the
most radical, shocking, and disturbing works of art, including works
whose avowed purpose is the demolition of the capitalist system itself.
Hence the seeming anomaly of The Sex Pistols' dadaesque brand of
anarchy, nihilism, violence, and pure noise being successfully marketed
in the United Kingdom and the United States. There have been
numerous other unusual and revealing examples. Derek Pell's darkly
humorous and bitingly satiric collage-and-text works (1977, 1978, 1981)
were brought out by Avon, a major New York publisher. Kathy Acker
gradually rose to literary stardom with a series of nightmarish punk

novels (1982, 1984, 1988, 1990) that are among the angriest and most graphic treatments of sexuality and violence published in the United States in this century. The film *Blue Velvet* (1986), Lynch's surreal and disturbing portrayal of the violence and sadomasochism that lies barely concealed beneath the bland surfaces of America's suburban dreams enjoyed commercial success. Performance artist and musician Laurie Anderson's success was equally unlikely, but her quirky blend of mini-malist music, stand-up comedy, fragmented lyrics of "found language," and odd instruments (a violin that "plays" human voices, a "vocoder" that electronically alters her voice) became popular concert attractions and best-selling albums (*Big Science* and *Mr. Heartbreak*), and films (*Home of the Brave*).[3]

The avant-pop phenomenon in literature has perhaps been best represented recently by the emergence of Mark Leyner. Leyner's uncon-ventional first book of surreal, dissolving stories, *I Smell Esther Williams*, went virtually unnoticed, but his equally unconventional second book, *My Cousin, My Gastroenterologist*, not only received raves from critics but transformed Leyner into a favorite among hip young readers. Al-though Leyner's work has been associated with the cyberpunk science fiction movement, *My Cousin* shares more with the nonhierarchical, rapid-fire, disjointed bits of images and information found on MTV than it does with any narrative form, even one as unconventional as cyber-punk. But for all its unconventionality, *My Cousin* speaks directly (via what Leyner refers to as "the violent vocabulary of the u.s.a.") to a generation of readers reared in the Media Age, in which just a flick of the switch will bring encounters with Ronald Reagan, Madonna, terror-ists hijacking a passenger plane, an ad for deodorant, *Voyager*'s photo-graphs of Neptune — all brought together as equals (and as equally "real") on the flattened screen of the television set.

Leyner's claim that his work should be considered realistic suggests how much both the literal and literary worlds have changed in the United States since the 1960s and 1970s, when the nontraditional fiction written by the first generation of postmodern authors (such as Pynchon, Barth, Sukenick, Donald Barthelme, Kurt Vonnegut, Robert Coover, and Raymond Federman) began to appear. These earlier authors had grown up during the 1940s and 1950s, and their aesthetic sensibili-ties were shaped by that period's notions of aesthetic innovation (for instance, the influence of the Beats, jazz, abstract expressionism, and the recent appearance in the United States of authors such as Franz Kafka,

Vladimir Nabokov, Samuel Beckett), even as they were attempting to free themselves from constrictive traditions existing in mainstream fiction. During the 1960s and early 1970s, they were producing fiction in the midst of a cultural, political, and aesthetic upheaval that was profoundly affecting everything from the way people dressed and looked (the casual, long-haired hippie style), to political attitudes concerning civil rights and the Vietnam War, to what people felt about drugs and sexual behavior. Inevitably, these changes in outer, public features and textures of daily American life were internalized and reflected in art that was equally unconventional and disruptive. Certainly in fiction this cultural turmoil was fully reflected not only in the vitality of the innovative novels and stories that were published between 1965 and 1975, but also in the impassioned debates among writers and critics that flourished about such issues as realism versus metafiction (and other experimentalist forms), moral versus "immoral" fiction, reflexive versus mimetic, and so on.

In the early 1990s, however, the cultural matrix that produced this first wave of postmodern fiction often seems as distant and old-fashioned as love beads, incense, and phrases like "Turn on, tune in, and drop out." And in fact, members of the new breed of American innovative writers are all demonstrating that American lives have been undergoing changes during the past twenty years that are every bit as "revolutionary" as what was taking place during the 1960s and early 1970s. This revolution has to do partially with demographic changes — for instance, with the massive yearly influx of Vietnamese, Cambodian, and particularly Mexican immigrants into our country, while the "native" population increasingly moves away from the older cities and neighborhoods of the Northeast and Midwest toward the southwestern and western states. It has to do with the political instability created by assassinations; the Vietnam War; scandals like Watergate, the Iran-contra affair, and the recent mind-boggling savings and loan debacle; the breakdown of totalitarian communist influences in the Soviet Union and eastern Europe; and the rise of Japan as a new economic rival and superpower. These events have all had the effect of radically undermining the American people's established notions about their goals and identity, their value systems, and where their country's interests (and enemies) lie.

But an even greater agent of change has been technology. Indeed, the most visible changes in Americans' daily lives are those involving information exchange (computers, fax and photocopy machines) and the saturation of people's daily lives with media-produced images and words. This saturation is encouraged not only by the greater ability of sophisticated advertisers to find means of bombarding individuals with their messages, but by the routine recording in people's homes of television shows, movies, music, and so forth on VCRs, audio cassettes, and the like, by humans interfacing with machines, and by startling developments in medicine, computer science, genetic engineering, chemistry. Such developments have also begun to change the way Americans think about the world and their relationship to it. For example, photography and VCRs have fundamentally altered our relationship to memory and the past generally. Likewise, postmodern theorists such as Jean Baudrillard, Arthur Kroker and David Cook, and Fredric Jameson have all argued that among the changes brought about by technology are the productions of what are, in effect, new kinds of realities. These are the "hyperrealities" and the worlds of the "simulacra" — those two-dimensional, infinitely seductive and reproducible worlds of the television or computer screen, of Disneyland and information exchange, the world of Reagan, Madonna, and Rambo. These are worlds that we interact with so regularly that they often seem fully as real as any other and have gradually begun to displace what used to be called "the real."

With such significant transformations taking place not only in our daily lives but in the basic categories we use to situate ourselves in these lives, it is not surprising that new American authors like Leyner, William Vollmann, James Boylan, and Don DeLillo have been mapping out a literary terrain very different from the landscapes created by writers even a generation before. They have responded to the "revolution" just outlined by producing a wide variety of forms, themes, and metaphors suitable for conveying a vivid and varied sense of the multiple realities now being inhabited by Americans. Indeed, what is likely to strike most readers is that American authors have apparently decided that no single underlying source of truth or realism is flexible enough to describe the myriad truths and realities that comprise American life today.

Thus, the realism found in the best recent American fiction is as likely to derive from dream or fantasy (as with Vollmann's *You Bright and Risen Angels* and Marianne Hauser's short story "The Seersucker Suit," or her novel *The Talking Room*) as from the gritty, ordinary lives of quiet desperation like those found in Raymond Carver's brilliant "minimalist" stories (1976, 1981, 1983). Sometimes, as in Ann Beattie's *Love Always* or Mark Laidlaw's *Dad's Nuke*, the world of television seems more real to the characters than the ordinary suburban world they seem to inhabit. On the other hand, the alienating but seductive daily world of America's "New South" depicted in Frederick Barthelme's works (1983, 1984, 1987) — a world of condominium living, endless shopping malls, and fast-food joints that literally didn't exist twenty years ago — seems every bit as artificial and fantastic as the television shows watched by his characters every night. Equally fantastic are the coked-out, fast-lane, but terribly lonely urban worlds evoked by "Brat Pack" novelists Jay McInerney (1984, 1988), Bret Ellis (1985), and Gibson (1984).

Contemporary novelists are, of course, living and writing during a period when media and computer worlds seem as substantial as any other. So it's hardly surprising that their fictional worlds are composed of a myriad of "reality sources." Some of the best recent novels are based on actual historical people and places. DeLillo's brilliant novel *Libra* recounts many of the events leading up to the assassination of John Kennedy from the perspective of Lee Harvey Oswald. William Kennedy's marvelous trilogy of novels (1975, 1978, 1983) focuses on Albany, New York, during the 1930s. Ron Hansen (1983) retells the story of the Wild West bandit Jesse James; Coover (1987) reincarnates Richard Nixon as a 1930s-era professional football player; and Vollmann's (1988) "New-New Journalism" paints portraits of San Francisco outcasts. But sources other than history or fact have also commonly been used to capture a sense of the reality of American life. Coover and Boylan transform familiar mythic incidents and figures drawn from films in *A Night At the Movies* and *Remind Me To Murder You Later*, respectively (see Boylan's "The Bride of Frankenstein"). Fairy tales and cartoons are retold in Max Apple's *The Oranging of America* and Coover's *In Bed One Night*; and various pop cultural forms are recycled by Leyner (1990), Jaffe (1987), and several of the stories in David Foster Wallace's collection (1989).

Paradoxically, some of most realistic descriptions of the "now" have been offered to us under the guise of glimpses into the future: Gibson's "cyberspace trilogy" (1984, 1986, 1988), Margaret Atwood's The Handmaid's Tale, and Bruce Sterling's *Islands in the Net* — or into the distant past: in Octavia Butler's *Kindred* and *Wild Seed*, Ron Hansen's *Desperadoes*, William S. Burroughs' *The Place of Dead Roads* and *Journey to the Western Lands*, Toni Morrison's *Beloved*, Samuel Delany's *Neveryon* series, and Vollmann's *The Ice-Shirt* — or by inventing alternate worlds whose history and reality at times intersect and at others diverge from what has occurred in our own world (see Russ 1975, Burroughs 1981, Piercy 1976, and Mooney 1981, 1990.

Meanwhile, "metafiction," in which the world of fiction or discourse itself is explored, continues to be a favorite mode for contemporary authors. Works such as Acker's series of "plagiarized" novels (1982, 1985, 1988, 1990); Russ' (1985) reflexive explorations of the underlying political, gender, and aesthetic implications of familiar science fiction motifs; and Derek Pell's marvelous deconstruction (1988) of the *Warren Commission Report*'s investigation into the Kennedy assassination all rely on the postmodern devices of pastiche, quotation, and appropriation of prior texts to generate new fiction that speaks to our own age. (For a slightly different approach to metafiction, see Vollmann's treatment of stories that Edgar Allen Poe *might have written* in "The Grave of Lost Stories.")

The point, then, is that with realities and world views proliferating exponentially, no single style, narrative perspective, or subject matter can lay claim to being the most realistic presentation of contemporary American life. Interestingly enough, the major trends in critical theory during the 1980s — poststructuralist, feminist, and neo-Marxist approaches — all stressed that truth, final meanings, and mimesis are always problematic terms, that hierarchies and privileged interpretations are culturally (and politically) determined rather than "natural" essences. These views, found in studies such as Brian McHale's *Postmodern Fiction*, Jameson's *The Political Unconscious*, Kroker and Cook's *The Postmodern Scene*, Marjorie Perloff's *The Poetics of Indeterminacy*, and Sandra Gilbert and Susan Gubar's *The Madwoman in the Attic* and *No Man's Land: The Place of the Woman Writer in the 20th Century*, reinforced and accounted for the variety of fictional modes that, while sharing the desire to "tell it like it is," possessed radically contradictory attitudes about the nature of this "telling," as well as what this "it" is that fiction was attempting to express.

With these general points in mind, I will devote the rest of this discussion to some observations about a few specific topics within recent American fiction that I feel are particularly noteworthy.

AMERICAN FICTION WRITER OF THE DECADE (1980–1990):
DON DeLILLO

DeLillo did not really emerge in the 1980s. His earlier work included the first important novel about rock music (1973) and football (1972); a major, encyclopedic novel (1976) in the excessive manner of William Gaddis and Pynchon; and several other novels that developed a wide variety of voices and genre conventions to explore a range of subjects like filmmaking, the drug culture, terrorism, espionage, and fanatical cults. But the three novels DeLillo published during the 1980s — *The Names*, *White Noise*, and *Libra* — collectively represent the most varied, innovative, and consistently perceptive exploration of contemporary American obsessions and culture to appear during this period.

The three novels are different in scope and method. *The Names* is a kind of international espionage or detective novel. *White Noise* uses a dystopian science fiction premise (an accidental release of toxic gas into an ordinary community) to delve into the central fears and joys of a society seeking comfort from shopping malls and distractions from television while it hides from death and absurdity. *Libra* depicts the ambiguous personalities and events that culminated in the now mythologized event that lies at the heart of the mystery of contemporary America — the assassination of Kennedy by Oswald. Looked at more closely, however, the three novels constantly circle around ultimacies — life and death, order and randomness, reason and irrationality, appearance and reality, the limits of language, the role of violence in a society allegedly devoted to peace. Broadly and darkly comic, created with a remarkable feel for the specific textures, idioms, and ambiguous resonances of daily life, the novels lay open the secret operations of American society in all its banality, blood, and beauty.

Other contenders: Coover (1981, 1986, 198x); Morrison (1981, 1987); T. C. Boyle (1981, 1984, 1985, 1987, 1989); Ursula Le Guin (1983, 1985, 1986); Paul Auster (1985, 1986, 1986, 1989, 1990); Acker (1982, 1984, 1986, 1988, 1990).

MOST IMPORTANT NEW "MAJOR" AMERICAN NOVELIST:
WILLIAM T. VOLLMANN

Like James Joyce, whose encyclopedic masterpieces, *Ulysses* and
Finnegans Wake, loomed large over the generation of modernist writers
who followed in his wake, Pynchon has cast an enormous and intimi-
dating shadow over the American authors who have emerged since the
1973 publication of *Gravity's Rainbow*. Throughout the 1980s, readers
and critics searched the literary horizons for a new talent of similarly
grand ambitions and originality. Occasional sightings were reported
throughout the decade: Boyle, John Calvin Batchelor (1980, 1983,
1985, 1990), David Foster Wallace (1987), Gibson (1984, 1986, 1988),
and Alexander Theroux (1981). But there was general agreement that
we hadn't yet seen a major new writer like Pynchon, who could knock
your socks off with his dazzling range of voices, topics, erudition, and
storytelling ability, while opening up new areas for narrative fiction.
  Enter William T. Vollmann.
  During the last few years, Vollmann has published in rapid succession three massive, unclassifiable, and utterly original works: *You Bright
and Risen Angels, The Rainbow Stories*, and *The Ice-Shirt*. Vollmann, who
draws the illustrations and maps for all his works, has also created a series
of remarkable "book art objects." (For example, *The Convict Bird*, a poem
about a woman in prison illustrated by Vollmann is encased in a steel
"cage" designed by industrial sculptor Matt Heckert of the Survival
Research Laboratories. *The Happy Girls*, in a 16'x20" format describes a
Thai brothel, with photographs by Ken Miller; the text, each page of
which is illustrated and hand-painted by Vollmann, is encased in a large
birchwood and mirror-glass box that contains a peephole, a buzzer that
activates a red lamp, and other oddities.) Four new Vollmann books
appeared by 1992: a collection, *13 Stories and 13 Epitaphs; Whores for
Gloria, or Everything Was Beautyiful Until the Girls Got Anixous*, a book
about prostitutes that contains Vollmann's most graphic and raw writing
to date; *An Afghanistan Picture Show*, based upon Vollmann's 1982
experiences entering Afghanistan with the rebels; and *Fathers and
Crows*, the sprawling second installment of Vollmann's septology of
"dream tales," which depicts the spiritually charged (and often extremely bloody) wars of belief between French Jesuits and the Iroquois
in North America between the sixteenth and eighteenth centuries.

The books published by Vollmann before 1991 share certain motifs, thematic concerns, and stylistic tendencies. All three, for example,
explore metamorphosis, the connection between sexuality and violence,
and the relationship between secret, inner histories and larger, public
ones. All tend to deal with characters who are outcasts, who have been
wounded in love and had that love change into hatred and violence. All
three use improvisatory methods, draw upon a myriad of meticulously
recorded data, and use Vollmann's own experiences interwoven with the
fictional materials he presents. The writing of these books has frequently
involved physical hardship and danger (secretly entering Afghanistan
with Islamic commandos; making solitary treks across the wilderness and
glaciers of Iceland, Greenland, and North Canada; spending time in San
Francisco's underworld of prostitutes and pimps, criminals, street people,
and drug dealers), another unifying feature that helps account for the
disturbing extremity of vision found in Vollmann's work.

Vollmann's books are fascinatingly different as well. *You Bright and
Risen Angels*, for example, is a wild, hallucinogenic depiction of the
failure of revolutionary impulses to overcome the reactionary forces of
greed, corruption, and violence that Vollmann feels have invaded the
American dream. Throughout *Angels* Vollmann adopts the voices and
perspectives of a bewildering variety of characters whose literal and
psychological beings are constantly being transformed into their primal
animal, insect, and vegetable essences. The book is somewhat reminiscent of Burroughs in its phantasmagoric descriptions of sex and violence,
and of Pynchon in its encyclopedic range of allusion and erudition and
its development of scientific metaphors (electricity functions in *Angels*
as entropy did in Pynchon's early works). But ultimately, what is most
notable about *Angels* is its originality: the ways Vollmann's darkly comic,
bizarre, and grotesque cartoon vision expresses so many aspects of
America's personal and mythic character; the disturbing power of its
presentations of sexual longings, loneliness, and betrayals; the sheer
energy of its extended flights of improvisational prose; and the relentless
honesty with which Vollmann presents himself.

Vollmann's second book, *The Rainbow Stories*, is a sequence of
interrelated tales about criminals, skinheads, prostitutes, derelicts, mur-
derers, and other lost souls that society trains us to hate or ignore.
Although most of the stories are based on actual encounters and interviews Vollmann had while he was living in San Francisco, others — such

as his retelling of the Shadrach, Meshach, and Abed-nego tale from the Old Testament in "Scintillant Orange" — draw their inspiration from earlier sources to develop startling parallels with the contemporary stories of loners and losers.

Vollmann's third novel, *The Ice-Shirt*, is the first of a seven-volume sequence of "dream" books that will eventually form a symbolic history of North America from its discovery a thousand years ago until the present. This first installment centers around the discovery of "Vinland" by tenth-century Norse explorers, their efforts over a period of three years to colonize this fertile but intractable wilderness, and their contacts with the native peoples that eventually result in their being attacked and driven out of North America.

But saying that *The Ice-Shirt* "centers" around anything basically distorts what Vollmann is up to here. The peculiar, fragmentary opening sections of the book, for example, recapitulate the 30,000-year history that produced the strange, red-bearded Norse tribe that felt compelled to leave the relative safety of northern Europe and ventured westward to Iceland, Greenland, and eventually North America. The colorful and passionate characters who appear later are all based on figures from Norse myth, sagas, and historical records; and the book is also embedded in the enormous amount of factual data gathered by Vollmann during travels to the Arctic, Greenland, Iceland, and Newfoundland. Finally, it is not these sources of information and history that Vollmann commands to "burst into flower" in his prolog. Instead, these sources are seeded by his imagination to produce a work whose spirit is playful and improvisational rather than literal-minded.

The Ice-Shirt, then, unfolds through a kaleidoscopic mixture of saga, obscure references and terminologies, vivid sensory details, modern travelog, and personal vignette. These features — combined with its five glossaries, a chronological table, dozens of pages of notes and sources, and numerous illustrations and maps — make for a reading experience as unduplicatable as that of Nabokov's *Pale Fire* or Le Guin's *Always Coming Home*. Gradually this prismatic method allows readers to make connections between different eras and methods of learning, between literal fact and symbolic truth. Ultimately the most significant "ice shirts" of the book's title are a symbol that suggests the cold hearts of the Norse explorers who first brought frost to a land once described as "Wineland the Good." This inner coldness brings with it a new heritage

of evil and impersonal violence, clearly linked by Vollmann to technology. It is a heritage that Vollmann apparently intends to pursue in the
remaining books of this grandly ambitious septology.

SCIENCE FICTION

One of the conclusions I came to in my *Columbia Literary History*
survey of recent American fiction, "The Fictions of the Present," was
that the most significant directions in recent American fiction include
"the emergence of science fiction (and its various hybrid forms) as a
major literary genre that has produced a body of work probably unrivaled
in stylistic versatility and thematic relevance" (p. 1162). That claim
seems even more evident to me today (and, in fact, this thesis lies at the
center of *Across the Wounded Galaxies*, a book of interviews I conducted
with a number of innovative and influential science fiction authors).
Indeed, given that postmodern American life can be seen as literally
being the life predicted by earlier generations of science fiction authors,
it is hardly surprising that recent authors of the genre are writing fiction
often particularly attuned to the brave new world(s) inhabited by
Americans in ways that traditional realistic works rarely do anymore.
Although the vast majority of American authors continue writing
fiction that basically ignores these realities, imaginative and stylistically
innovative science fiction authors such as Gregory Benford, Octavia
Butler, Samuel R. Delany, Thomas Disch, William Gibson, Ursula Le
Guin, Joanna Russ, Bruce Sterling, and Gene Wolfe (all interviewed in
Wounded Galaxies) have been producing fiction that explores the personal, social, and philosophical aspects of postmodern culture with
considerable boldness. Because much of this writing is so radical and
formally experimental, and because writing that bears the imprint of
science fiction has been so commonly relegated to pulp ghettoes, science
fiction has until recently remained largely ignored and unremarked upon
(except within the relatively insular world of genre science fiction).
Some of the most intense and appreciative responses to science
fiction from outside the genre have come from feminist readers and
critics, who were quick to recognize the radical, often highly politicized
implications of the works of such female science fiction authors as Le
Guin, Russ, Butler, James Tiptree Jr. (Alice Sheldon), Suzy Charnas,
Suzette Elgin, Kate Wilhelm, and Vonda McIntrye. Nor was it accidental

that so many women from outside science fiction chose to write science fiction or quasi–science fiction works during this period (examples would include Atwood's *The Handmaid's Tale*, Piercy's *Woman on the Edge of Time*, Doris Lessing's *Shikasta* series, Carol Hill's *Eleven Million Mile High Dancer*, Acker's *Empire of the Senseless*, and Angela Carter's *The Passion of New Eve*). The sources of science fiction's appeal for feminists should be fairly obvious. Its elasticity as a genre allows women who are interested in gender issues (and those social, political, linguistic, and cultural issues that immediately arise from and attach themselves to gender issues) to invent alien worlds specifically tailored to highlight those issues; to peer into earth's future and project likely developments of current attitudes; and to juxtapose alternate universes with our own for the purposes of examining contemporary gender roles — and their possible alternatives.

"SLIPSTREAM" FICTION AND CYBERPUNK

Writers working at the boundaries of science fiction and postmodern experimentalism are increasingly borrowing the motifs, language, symbols, images — as well as the "subject matter" — of science fiction to produce hybrid works that Bruce Sterling recently dubbed "slipstream novels."[4] This process began in the United States back in the 1950s and early 1960s, when literary mavericks like Pynchon, Burroughs, Alfred Bester, J. G. Ballard, Kurt Vonnegut, Jr., and Philip K. Dick began publishing books that self-consciously operated on the fringes of science ficiton and the literary avant-garde. It accelerated throughout the 1970s and 1980s with the publication of such important examples as DeLillo's *Ratner's Star* and *White Noise*, Hauser's *The Talking Room*, Mooney's *East Travel to Other Planets*, Denis Johnson's *Fiskadoro*, Rachel Ingalls' *Mrs. Caliban*, Steve Erickson's *Days Between Stations* and *Rubicon Beach*, Joseph McElroy's *Plus* and *Women and Men*, Federman's *The Twofold Vibration*, Stephen Wright's *M-31: A Family Romance*, Acker's *Empire of the Senseless*, Vollmann's *You Bright and Risen Angels*, and Leyner's *My Cousin, My Gastroenterologist*. Although outside the commercial science fiction publishing scene, these writers all produced works that perfectly fulfill the generic task of science fiction, described by Vivian Sobchack (1988) as "the cognitive mapping and poetic figuration of social relations as these are constituted by new technological modes of "being-in-the-world" (p. 225). As is true of the cyberpunk novels that began appearing in the mid-1980s[5] — such as Gibson's *Neuromancer*, Mark Laidlaw's *Dad's Nuke*, Sterling's *Schizmatrix* and *Islands in the Net*, and John Shirley's *Eclipse* trilogy — these slipstream novels typically portrayed individuals awash in a sea of technological change, information overload, and random — but extraordinarily vivid — sensory stimulations. Personal confusion, sadness, dread, and philosophical skepticism often appeared mixed with equal measures of euphoria and nostalgia for a past when centers could still hold. The characters and events in these works typically existed within a narrative framework that reached its most extreme expression early on: in Burroughs' hallucinatory mid-1960s trilogy, *The Soft Machine*, *The Ticket That Exploded*, and *Nova Express*. A few of these mainstream postmodern writers have drawn very self-consciously from genre science fiction norms for specific tropes and narrative devices. This is very obvious, for example, in Burroughs' use of the motifs of the 1930s "space opera" pulp novels he read as a youth, in DeLillo's borrowing of dystopian elements in *White Noise*, in Vollmann's improvisational treatment of a much wider range of science fiction modes in *You Bright and Risen Angels*, and in Acker's borrowings of specific passages from *Neuromancer* in *Empire of the Senseless*. But usually one sees less and less of these authors consciously borrowing from genre science fiction norms than of their introducing these elements simply because the world around them demands that the elements be present.

MULTICULTURAL FICTION IN A MULTICULTURAL SOCIETY

The impressive vitality and variety of writing published by gay men and women, African-Americans, Native Americans, Mexican-Americans, Asian-Americans, Caribbean-Americans, and other minority groups in the United States recently has been yet another factor contributing to the more flexible notions of literary realism that characterize contemporary American fiction. American writers who emerge from ethnic minority backgrounds or the gay community have often been reared in worlds very different from those of the straight white majority. They have grown up with different standards of living, frequently in communities isolated from the "mainstream." Often they have different cultural habits, different ways of thinking, different values and myths, different social customs and ways of expressing their sexuality and their anger. Often they speak a different language, or a variation of English possessing its own accent and exotic idioms.

Largely ignored by America's commercial publishing industry until recently — unless they were willing to tell their stories using narrative and cultural assumptions that the straight white world could easily accept — these ethnic and sexual minority authors have, during the past fifteen years, begun to find publishing outlets that permit them to tell their own stories in their own ways by embedding their works within their own cultural idioms and myths. Several of these works rank as among the most original and imaginative works in American fiction. Morrison powerfully and movingly depicts the effects of slavery in nineteenth-century America. Maxine Hong Kingston's trio of novels (1976, 1980, 1989) juxtaposes the experiences of Chinese-Americans adapting to life in the United States with the myths, fairy tales, and "talk stories" of their Chinese heritage. Lesbian feminist Russ (1975) literal-izes the notion that marginalized people live in different worlds by using the science fiction alternate world premise; here Russ presents a woman (bearing a certain resemblance to Russ herself) who encounters three alternative selves from other universes — a woman from a feminist utopia, a woman from a brutal, radically patriarchal world, and a woman from a world in which gender conflicts have escalated into armed violence. Leslie Marmon Silko (1980) allows the different aspects of her life (the tribal myths and legends she grew up with, photographs, personal anecdotes, and stories she's invented) to interact with one another until they slowly coalesce into a unified portrait of herself — the "storyteller" of the book's title. Octavia Butler (1979) casts a strong, adaptable black woman back to the early days of slavery in pre–Civil War America — a simple but suggestive vehicle for developing contrasts and comparisons between our own age's racial and political assumptions and those of earlier eras.

These gay and ethnic writers all tend to tell their version of "how it is" in the multicultural world of America by embedding their descrip-tions of ordinary life in the context of their own customs, slang, and world view. These books, like the others I have been discussing, refuse to privilege a single familiar world; instead they insist that reality is multiple, a fluid interaction of people, codes, and meanings not reduc-ible to the empirical biases of most so-called realistic fiction of the past. This interaction, like the interactions I referred to earlier between avant-garde and pop culture, between science fiction and mainstream fiction, and between the fantastic and the mundane, has been producing a body of American fiction that takes nothing for granted. If it has not yet reached the idealized "everything is permitted" status envisioned by Hasan i-Sabbah, it has at least made a major move in that direction. That status is one of open-endedness, imaginative and creative freedom, and the recognition that no single world — literary or otherwise — has the right to impose its will over others. It is a state, in short, that has always been at the heart of the American ideal, but which in the world of fiction has too often been ignored.

NOTES

1. Among the most useful descriptions of "postmodernism" are McHale, Kroker and Cook, McCaffery, and — probably the single most provocative and useful discussion — Jameson.

2. See, for example, the extended discussions of this merging of categories in McHale, McCaffery, Hedbidge, and Jameson.

3. Anderson, whose work has been majorly influenced by William S. Burroughs, played a role in the remarkable transformation of Burroughs from a renegade "outlaw" artist-figure during the 1960s into a pop star by having Burroughs perform with her in some of her shows and in her concert movie, *Home of the Brave*. That Burroughs, probably the most extreme and brilliant fictional innovator in the United States since the Second World War, has become a pop icon is the most striking example of the "avant-pop" phenomenon of them all.

4. See Sterling's essay, which includes a comprehensive list of slipstream novels.

5. The cyberpunk science fiction movement was unquestionably the most significant development in the field of genre science fiction during the 1980s. Sparked initially by the publication of Gibson's *Neuromancer* in 1984, and gathering momentum through the series of public debates in science fiction publications and at science fiction conferences throughout the mid-1980s, cyberpunk represented a "break-through" in science fiction similar to the breakthrough created by the punk movement in rock music during the 1970s. In many ways, cyberpunk can be seen as representing the postmodernization of science fiction, just as back in the 1960s science fiction had gone through its modernism phase when the New Wave science fiction movement consciously began to graft modernist experimentalist methods (of, for example, James Joyce, William Faulkner, and John Dos Passos) onto science fiction narratives. For a more thorough look at cyberpunk and its relationship to postmodernism, see my introduction to a special edition of *Mississippi Review*, as well as the other materials collected in that cyberpunk "casebook." A much expanded version of this casebook has been published as *Storming the Reality Studio: A Casebook*

of Cyberpunk and Postmodern Science Fiction, Larry McCaffrey, ed. Durham: Duke University Press, 1991.

WORKS CITED

Acker, Kathy. 1982. *Empire of the Senseless.* New York: Grove Press.

———. 1984. *Blood and Guts in High School.* New York: Grove Press.

———. 1985. *Don Quixote.* New York: Grove Press.

———. 1988. *Great Expectations.* New York: Grove Press.

———. 1989. *My Death, My Life by Pier Paolo Pasolini.* New York: Grove Press.

———. 1990. *In Memoriam to Identity.* New York: Grove Press.

Apple, Max. 1976. *The Oranging of America.* New York: Grossman Publishers.

Atwood, Margaret. 1981. *The Handmaid's Tale.* New York: Ballentine.

Auster, Paul. 1985. *City of Glass.* Los Angeles: Sun and Moon Press.

———. 1986. *Ghosts.* Los Angeles: Sun and Moon Press.

———. 1986. *The Locked Room.* Los Angeles: Sun and Moon Press.

———. 1989. *Moon Palace.* New York: Viking Press.

———. 1990. *The Music of Chance.* New York: Viking Press.

Barthelme, Frederick. 1983. *Moon Deluxe.* New York: Simon and Schuster.

———. 1984. *Second Marriage.* New York: Simon and Schuster.

———. 1987. *Tracer.* New York: Simon and Schuster.

Batchelor, John Calvin. 1980. *The Further Adventures of Halley's Comet.* New York: St. Martin's.

———. 1983. *The Birth of the People's Republic of Antarctica.* New York: Dial Press.

———. 1985. *American Falls.* New York: Norton.

———. 1990. *Gordon Liddy Is My Muse.* New York: Linden Press.

Baudrillard, Jean. 1983. *Simulations.* New York: Semiotext(e).

Beattie, Ann. 1986. *Love Always.* New York: Random House.

Boylan, James. 1988. *Remind Me To Murder You Later.*

Boyle, T. C. 1981. *Water Music.* Boston: Little, Brown.

———. 1984. *Budding Prospects.* New York: Viking.

———. 1985. *Greasy Lake and Other Stories.* New York: Viking.

———. 1987. *World's End.* New York: Viking.

———. 1989. *If the River Was Whiskey.* New York: Viking.

Burroughs, William S. 1964. *Nova Express.* New York: Grove Press.

———. 1966. *The Soft Machine*. New York: Grove Press.

———. 1967. *The Ticket That Exploded*. New York: Grove Press.

———. 1981. *Cities of the Red Night*. New York: Holt, Rinehart and Winston.

———. 1983. *The Place of Dead Roads*. New York: Holt, Rinehart and Winston.

———. 1986. *Journey to the Western Lands*. New York: Viking.

Butler, Octavia. 1979. *Kindred*. Garden City, NY: Doubleday.

———. 1980. *Wild Seed*. Garden City, NY: Doubleday.

Carter, Angela. 1977. *The Passion of New Eve*. New York: Harcourt, Brace, Jovanovich.

Carver, Raymond. 1976. *Will You Please Be Quiet, Please?* New York: McGraw-Hill.

———. 1981. *What We Talk About When We Talk About Love*. New York: Vintage.

———. 1983. *Cathedral*. New York: Alfred A. Knopf.

Coover, Robert. 1981. *Spanking the Maid*. New York: Grove Press.

———. 1983. *In Bed One Night*. Providence, RI: Burning Deck Press.

———. 1986. *Gerald's Party*. New York: Linden Press/Simon and Schuster.

———. 1987. *A Night at the Movies*. New York: Linden Press/Simon and Schuster.

———. 1987. *Whatever Happened to Gloomy Gus of the Chicago Bears?* New York: Linden Press/Simon and Schuster.

DeLillo, Don. 1972. *End Zone*. Boston: Houghton-Mifflin.

———. 1973. *Great Jones Street*. Boston: Houghton-Mifflin.

———. 1976. *Ratner's Star*. New York: Alfred A. Knopf.

———. 1982. *The Names*. New York: Alfred A. Knopf.

———. 1985. *White Noise*. New York: Viking.

———. 1988. *Libra*. New York: Viking.

Ellis, Bret Easton. 1985. *Less Than Zero*. New York: Simon and Schuster.

Erickson, Steve. 1985. *Days Between Stations*. New York: Poseidon Press.

———. 1985. *Rubicon Beach*. New York: Poseidon Press.

Federman, Raymond. 1982. *The Twofold Vibration*. Bloomington: Indiana University Press.

Gibson, William. 1984. *Neuromancer*. New York: Berkley Press.

———. 1986. *Burning Chrome*. New York: Arbor House.

———. 1986. *Count Zero*. New York: Arbor House.

———. 1988. *Mona Lisa Overdrive*. New York: Bantam.

Gilbert, Sandra, and Susan Gubar. 1979. *The Madwoman in the Attic*. New Haven: Yale University Press.

———. 1987. *No Man's Land: The Place of the Woman Writer in the Twentieth Century*. New Haven: Yale University Press.

Hansen, Ron. 1979. *Desperadoes*. New York: Alfred A. Knopf.

———. 1983. *The Assassination of Jessee James by the Coward Robert Ford*. New York: Alfred A. Knopf.

Hauser, Marianne. 1975. *The Talking Room*. New York: Fiction Collective.

Hebdige, Dick. 1979. *Subculture, the Meaning of Style*. New York: Methuen.

Hill, Carol. 1985. *The Eleven Million Mile High Dancer*. New York: Holt, Rinehart and Winston.

Ingalls, Rachel. 1983. *Mrs. Caliban*. New York: Dell.

Jaffe, Harold. 1987. *Madonna and Other Spectacles*. New York: PAJ Press.

Jameson, Fredric. 1983. *The Political Unconscious*. Ithaca, NY: Cornell University Press.

———. 1984. "Postmodernism, or the Cultural Logic of Late Capitalism." *New Left Review* 146 (July-Aug 1984): 53–94.

Johnson, Denis. 1985. *Fiskadoro*. New York: Alfred A. Knopf.

Kennedy, William. 1975. *Legs*. New York: Penguin Books.

———. 1978. *Billy Phelan's Greatest Game*. New York: Penguin Books.

———. 1983. *Ironweed*. New York: Viking.

Kingston, Maxine Hong. 1977. *Woman Warrior*. New York: Vintage Books.

———. 1980. *China Man*. New York: Alfred A. Knopf.

———. 1989. *Tripmaster Monkey*. New York: Alfred A. Knopf.

Krokee, Arthur, and David Cook. 1986. *The Postmodern Scene: Excremental Culture of Hyperaesthetics*. New York: St. Martin's Press.

Laidlaw, Mark. 1984. *Dad's Nuke*. New York: Lorevan.

Le Guin, Ursula. 1983. *The Compass Rose*. New York: Harper and Row.

———. 1985. *Always Coming Home*. New York: Harper and Row.

———. 1986 *Buffalo Gals*. Santa Barbara: Capra Press.

Leyner, Mark. 1983. *I Smell Esther Williams*. New York: Fiction Collective.

———. 1990. *My Cousin, My Gastroenterologist*. New York: Harmony/Crown.

McCaffery, Larry. 1986. *Postmodern Fiction: A Bio-Bibliographical Guide*. Westport, CT: Greenwood Press.

———. 1988. "The Fictions of the Present." In *The Columbia University History of the United States*. Ed. Emory Elliot. New York: Columbia University Press, pp. 1161–79.

———. 1990. *Across the Wounded Galaxies: Interviews with Contemporary American Science Fiction Authors*. Urbana, IL: University of Illinois Press.

McElroy, Joseph. 1977. *Plus*. New York: Alfred A. Knopf.

———. 1987. *Women and Men*. New York: Alfred A. Knopf.

McHale, Brian. 1987. *Postmodern Fiction*. New York: Methuen.

McInerney, Jay. 1984. *Bright Lights, Big City*. New York: Vintage Contemporaries.

————. 1988. *Story of My Life*. New York: Atlantic Monthly Press.

Mooney, Ted. 1981. *Easy Travel to Other Planets*. New York: Farrar, Straus, Giroux.

————. 1990. *Traffic and Laughter*. New York: Alfred A. Knopf.

Morrison, Toni. 1981. *Tar Baby*. New York: Alfred A. Knopf.

————. 1987. *Beloved*. New York: Alfred A. Knopf.

Nabokov, Vladimir. 1962. *Pale Fire*. New York: Putnam.

Pell, Derek. 1977. *Dr. Bey's Suicide Handbook*. New York: Dodd Mead and Co.

————. 1978. *Dr. Bey's Handbook of Strange Sex*. New York: Avon.

————. 1981. *Dr. Bey's Book of the Dead*. New York: Avon.

————. 1983. *Morbid Curiosities*. London: Jonathan Cape.

————. 1988. *Assassination Rhapsody*. New York: Semiotext(e).

Perloff, Marjorie. 1981. *The Poetics of Indeterminacy*. Princeton, NJ: Princeton University Press.

Piercy, Marge. 1976. *Woman on the Edge of Time*. New York: Alfred A. Knopf.

Pynchon, Thomas. 1973. *Gravity's Rainbow*. New York: Viking.

Russ, Joanna. 1975. *The Female Man*. Boston: Gregg.

————. 1985. *Extra(ordinary) People*. New York: St. Martin's Press.

Silko, Leslie Marmon. 1981. *Storyteller*. New York: Seaver Books.

Sterling, Bruce. 1985. *Schismatrix*. New York: Arbor House.

————. 1988. *Islands in the Net*. New York: Morrow.

Sukenick, Ronald. 1987. *Down and In: Life in the Underground*. New York: Morrow.

Theroux, Alexander. 1981. *Darconville's Cat*. Garden City, NY: Doubleday.

Vollmann, William T. 1987. *You Bright and Risen Angels*. New York: Vintage.

————. 1988. *The Convict Bird*. San Francisco: CoTangent Press.

————. 1988. *The Rainbow Stories*. New York: Macmillan.

————. 1990. *The Happy Girls*. San Francisco: CoTangent Press.

————. 1990. *The Ice-Shirt*. New York: Viking.

————. 1992. *An Afghanistan Picture Show*. New York: Farrar, Straus, Giroux.

————. 1992. *Fathers and Crows*. New York: Viking.

————. 1992. *Thirtees Stories, Thirteen Epitaphs*. London: Andre Deutsch.

————. 1992. *Whores for Gloria*. New York: Pantheon.

Wallace, David Foster. 1989. *The Girl with the Curious Hair*. New York: W. W. Norton.

Wright, Stephen. 1988. *M-31: A Family Romance*. New York: Harmony Books.

A Comparative View of Mexican Fiction in the Seventies

JOHN S. BRUSHWOOD, *University of Kansas*

The fiction of the 1970s in Mexico might be described as fascinating, hard to read, technically intricate, elitist, sophisticated, intellectually stimulating, self-conscious, and more. Because history has not yet placed contemporary literature in a perspective where we may view it comfortably, critics are often tempted to compensate by qualifying their statements too elaborately. In order to be as clear as possible, I shall divide my observations into three sections: (1) a general view — the image — of Mexican fiction of the 1970s, (2) the apparent function of the novel during the late 1960s and 1970s, and (3) indications of changes taking place in fiction of the late 1970s.

THE IMAGE OF THE CONTEMPORARY MEXICAN NOVEL

The image of the Mexican novel during the 1970s may be described by commenting first on some writers and then on certain tendencies. Obviously, I am not planning to mention all the novelists who have been active, but a selected few may serve as indicators.

There can be no doubt that Carlos Fuentes is the best known of this group. He has long been recognized as one of the novelists of the Spanish-American "boom" and is also known for his speculation on the nature of fiction. His novel *Terra Nostra* (1975) is a gigantic recasting of history in which Fuentes searches out the meaning of Spain in America. The novel is forbidding because of its size and the relative impenetrability of its narrative structure. On the other hand, it has to be regarded as a major work by a highly gifted writer. It is an important part of the author's identification of reality. He is and has always been obsessed by history. *Terra Nostra* is also a fiction that is about fiction, because it interrelates established fictional characters — for example, Don Juan, Celestina — with Fuentes' own invented characters and transformations of historical personages.

Fuentes is by now one of Mexico's older novelists. If we look among younger writers of the 1970s for someone with a substantial body of work, an established reputation, and a promising future, we find Gustavo Sainz. Along with José Agustín, Sainz initiated the fiction of *la onda* — the younger generation of the 1960s whose members flaunted their disrespect for conventionalities, and especially for the inhibitions placed on language by social custom. His first four novels are quite different from each other in many ways, but they do share two constants: the author's sensitivity to language and an equally sharp awareness of the city as his home. He is a novelist of the city — not in the sense of a writer who has come from the provinces and discovered the exotic and disturbing ways of the capital, but in the sense of a writer for whom Mexico City is the native region, the place where he grew up and in which his identity is rooted.

The novels of Fuentes and Sainz are particularly noteworthy for their innovations in narrative technique, and they sometimes inspire questions about whether there are Mexican authors writing novels in more familiar forms. Without going into the very complicated issue suggested by this query, I can say that there are probably books in Mexico that would be readily identified as "character novels," with no disturbing caveats added. Sergio Galindo is one of several authors writing in this form. To place this information in a context that permits a rough comparison — I hope without creating grave misconceptions — if Fuentes and Sainz might correspond to Thomas Pynchon or John Barth, Galindo and others like him might correspond to Graham Greene or Bernard Malamud.

Certainly the authors of character novels are much less generally known than their more innovative contemporaries. However, it would be dangerous to assume a correlation between innovation and high profile, because there are some very strange Mexican novels written by relatively little known authors. I think of Salvador Elizondo as an example. One way of describing the work of these writers is to say that certain notions form the basis of their novels, and what we remember after reading one of them is the development of the notion rather than the development of characters. However, if we extend slightly the boundaries around this group, it would be possible to say that their production ranges from an approximation of the French *nouveau roman* to a metafiction suggestive of John Barth's *Chimera*.

If we think in terms of tendencies in the novel, rather than of authors, it is possible to point out the distinguishing characteristics of the genre during the 1970s. I will often mention technical innovation, but I do not mean that this kind of inventiveness belongs only to one period of ten years. Indeed, the fiction of the Mexican Jaime Torres Bodet and others — some of it written almost a half-century ago — uses techniques that have been present in fiction since Marcel Proust and James Joyce but are still considered, occasionally, to be new. It is also apparent that Agustín Yáñez's *Al filo del agua* (*The Edge of the Storm*) in 1947 reasserted the novelist's right to create rather than paint a true-to-life portrait of a social condition. Since approximately 1962, the novel of the "boom" has certainly used a wide variety of narrative techniques and obviously enjoyed playing with language. Nevertheless, it seems to me that the tendency does not stop at this point. By 1967, technical wizardry reached a level of virtuosity where the narrative procedure dominated all other aspects of some works. Such virtuosity was accompanied by a tide of allusions, many of them necessarily unfamiliar to a large number of readers. The result was an "in" type of novel that made a few readers feel very cozy and the larger public very unwelcome.

The exclusiveness of these novels emphasizes the authors' interest in observing the art of creating fiction. Claude Fell, a French critic of Latin American literature, noted this characteristic in 1970 among new tendencies of the novel and cited Elizondo's *El hipogeo secreto* (1968) as an example.[1] The authors' fascination (Fell's word) need not refer only to novels in which the phenomenon is as dominant as it is in Elizondo's novel. There are many in which it is apparent to varying extents. These books are fictions that are about fictions. We may call them metafictions; but it is well to remember that a novel may have a metafictional aspect along with other characteristics, and the relative importance of the metafictional aspect may vary from one work to another.

THE FUNCTION OF THE NOVEL DURING THE PERIOD
1967–1977

When we recognize these tendencies as characteristic of Mexican fiction during a period of ten years, it is possible to point out some further developments that may indicate a different function of the novel. However, we cannot deal with these developments clearly without examining first some aspects of the meaning of the novel during the period 1967–1977. I shall divide this section of my comments into three parts: (1) the ambivalent reaction of readers, (2) the function of the novel as an artistic experience, and (3) the effect of the novel on readers after the book has been read.

The novel has been following an exclusivistic route that delights a select group of readers and displeases many others. Why does this conflict exist? I am not concerned here with the problem of how large an audience art should seek. Rather, I am simply recognizing an obvious fact — that many people who enjoyed reading new novels a few years ago do not read them anymore. Corollary to this fact is the presence in bookstores of large numbers of books often referred to as nonfiction. These treatises explain how to do something or promise solutions to the problems of the world or of individuals. They may or may not keep the promise, but many copies are sold. More stimulating to the imagination are biographies, memoirs, and essays on strange natural or historical phenomena. Thinking of the works of nonfiction in general, I suspect that readers seek in them some assurance of stability, some promise that they may discover a right way, some identification with other humans who have "made it."

There must be a relationship between this preference and the frequent references to "traditional" novels or "understandable" novels. These terms are heard in the remarks of quite literate people. I am not searching out the reactions of people who do not enjoy reading. The problem has to do with the representation of reality. More than forty years ago, an eminent scholar, Erich Auerbach, wrote his now classic study on the representation of reality in Western literature.[2] Toward the end of this work, he has to take account of Joyce's *Ulysses* and other novels in which various aspects of reality are so fragmented that, for a reader attuned to the nineteenth-century novel, they seem to offer no representation of reality at all. Chronologically, *Ulysses* is a long way from the recent Mexican novels I have been referring to; but it may be considered the beginning of the problem I am dealing with now.

Auerbach notes the relationship of this kind of fiction to the nature of social reality following the First World War. Reality was itself fragmented, disjointed, hard to comprehend. Although he recognizes this relationship of the new fiction to the new reality, Auerbach is so concerned for an older kind of representation that he cannot let the Joycean novel go without censure. His exact words are important:

> There is something confusing, something hazy about them, something hostile to the reality which they represent. We not infrequently find a turning away from the practical will to live, or delight in portraying it under its most brutal forms. There is hatred of culture and civilization, brought out by means of the subtlest stylistic devices which culture and civilization have developed, and often a radical and fanatical urge to destroy.[3]

Frustrated or weary readers of recent fiction frequently make statements similar to Auerbach's, usually in a less elegant fashion. It is worth noting, however, that Auerbach's discomfort is caused not only by the narrative technique, but by the author's attitude as well. Or if we assume that this attitude reflects reality, Auerbach does not like reality. It is impossible to estimate the extent to which contemporary readers may dislike the *kind* of reality recent fiction portrays.[4] On the other hand, it is easy to see that they, like Auerbach, often find current novels confusing and hazy.

The objection seems to be composed of three interrelated factors: (1) the change from nineteenth-century realism forces readers into unfamiliar territory; (2) some postrealist novels make use of many allusions that may be unfamiliar to some readers, either because the allusions are recondite or because they belong to the intimate world of the author and his friends; and (3) readers are expected to commit themselves to the work in ways that cause them to participate more and observe less than in a novel of realism. Obviously, the narrative techniques of the postrealist novel do provide a special kind of experience, and it is equally apparent that part of the objection may be explained by the fact that change requires a period of adjustment. *Ulysses* no longer evokes the outcry of fifty years ago. Juan Rulfo's *Pedro Páramo* is an old standby. Multiple narrative voices in William Faulkner's *The Sound and the Fury* still make interesting analyses possible, but the phenomenon is no longer disconcerting. Nevertheless, in all these novels the reader is required to participate in some way in the organization of the material. The degree of such participation, the frequency with which fiction reading requires it, and the skill of the author in evoking it — these three seem to be the factors that govern the intensity of reaction to such novels.

With respect to the function of the novel, Robert Scholes and Robert Kellogg have said that "we can hazard the notion that stories appeal primarily because they offer a simulacrum of life which enables an audience to participate in events without being involved in the consequences which events in the actual world would inevitably carry with them."[5] Such appeal indicates the appreciation of an experience that the reader may live vicariously, or reject, or even judge. However, in the metafictional novels, the reader's relationship to the narrative situation changes substantially. It is important to point out that readers are not always involved by subtle means. They may be overtly challenged to write the novel. In *Lapsus* (1971), Héctor Manjarrez interrupts the narration to suggest that readers might wish to write a certain kind of episode at that point. After suggesting a source of inspiration for such a contribution, the narrator continues: "Even better, the reader may, if he wishes, imagine any kind of episode he might like, so long as he doesn't leave Huberto goofing off in his easy chair."[6] Obviously, this contact between narrator and reader plays havoc with the experience described by Scholes and Kellogg. It suggests a feigned detachment on the part of the storyteller. However, it is equally possible that the writer may be confronting a vital problem in contemporary fiction. Let us consider a statement by Pere Gimferrer in an essay on Fuentes' *Terra Nostra*. The critic says the essential question that paralyzes narrative in our time is: why narrate this rather than that, or simply, why narrate?[7] He also says that one of Fuentes' major achievements is the incorporation of this question into the very structure of the novel. Something similar might be said with respect to José Emilio Pacheco's *Morirás lejos* (1967), in which the interrelationship of alternatives becomes most important and thus subordinates theme and obliterates character identity.

My comments on these novels are not intended to be derogatory. The point is to demonstrate that their function is different from the function anticipated by many readers whose reactions I know. In any conceivable communication act, someone sends a message to someone else. If the person who receives the message becomes also the one who sends the message, we have the equivalent of someone talking to him/herself. In terms of the novel, if readers become narrators, they are making the fiction for themselves, inventing the happening they wish to experience vicariously.[8] There is no reason why such a procedure cannot happen; however, I am not persuaded that many people wish to participate in it more than once or twice.

Awareness of fiction in the making is most intense in novels where the story is actually the creation of the story. We might say that the perfect fiction is one that generates a subordinate fiction in such a way that both the primary fiction and the subordinate fiction have the same outcome. John Barth apparently thinks along this line in the writing of *Chimera*. Elizondo's *El hipogeo secreto* might be described as a novel in which the narrator and the reader gradually become one. Vicente Leñero's *El garabato* (1967) deals with inventions inside inventions that all lead in the same direction. Interesting fictional constructions, but are they about anything? Of course, they are about creating fictions.

There is a difference between the experience of reading a novel and the effect of the novel on a reader after the book is read. The latter amounts to a kind of interpretation of the work. In general, what we remember of metafiction novels is the clever idea — or maybe only the technique itself. Such emphasis on technique, extrapolated to the world in which the reader lives, immediately suggests the enormous number of "how-to" books that are available. Even closer to us who are gathered in the academic situation is the practice of spending hours on procedural matters — in committees, assemblies, senates, conferences — hours spent on how to do something that seem quite out of proportion to the hours spent in taking substantive action.

If narrative techniques may be related to worldly reality in this regard, it is equally interesting to explore the significance of a two-step invention, or the invention of invention.[9] One step is the transformation of the anecdotal material — the development of the basic material into plot. If this basic material is related in any way to the reality in which the novelist lives, the novelist's narrative act transforms that reality into a literary experience. However, if a subordinate fiction is invented within this act of transformation, it is a creative act removed by an additional step from the basic material. This procedure may well correspond to a tendency in society to invent a subordinate problem that will absorb our attention and protect us from facing a basic problem that we cannot solve or may not wish to solve.

Lest we be tempted to put aside these possibilities as unlikely, let us recall that the novels are very real. They do exist, and it is impossible to demonstrate convincingly that any work of art is totally separated from the human milieu in which it is created. It is far easier to show that literature has sought to adjust its expression to accommodate changes in the reality that it has sought to represent. Auerbach's study states the case eloquently. Even when he boggles before Joyce, Auerbach recognizes the possible correspondence of the new expression to a new reality. In fact, from the time of Joyce up to the present, we may observe a new reality, a new perception of reality, and a new way of expressing it. Like Auerbach, many may not wish to recognize that reality. On the other hand, we must not assume that alienation from contemporary fiction necessarily means flight from the fragmented reality of our time.[10] We have already noted certain narrative procedures that distort the generally accepted act of communication.

The most disturbing aspect of reader alienation is the loss of aesthetically creative activity. Hardly anyone would deny that we live in a situation that needs an increase of such activity, not a decrease. In the best imaginable reader-novel relationship, the kind of fiction I refer to probably enhances the creative participation of readers. However, if it reduces the number of readers, we must question its value to a society that needs help in expressing itself. Those who read metafiction profitably are those who are able to accept the unusual narrator-reader role — or at least suspend a negative reaction to it — and so enjoy the act itself rather than rely on a message of some kind. Others must find themselves abdicating the more traditional role (possibly less creative, but nonetheless important) that they may well have considered their right.

INDICATIONS OF POSSIBLE CHANGES

More than a few people have asked me — and I am sure many others have been asked the same question — whether I expect a return to a more accessible kind of fiction. In the mid-1970s, my response tended to be affirmative. However, the question is not as straightforward as it seems, and an answer is not simple. In the first place, there is plenty of accessible fiction being written. Some of it is not very artistic, but much of it is quite recommendable. The other necessary clarification has to do with plot. When people complain about the absence of a story, it is hard to believe they are talking about recent fiction. Metafiction is nothing but story.

Jorge Luis Borges, one of the greatest storytellers of all time, has been a major influence in the renaissance of plot invention. However, concentration on fiction for the sake of making a fiction tends to decrease the importance of characterization with which the reader can identify. In fact, metafiction may reasonably be considered a reaction against the agonized character studies of a few years earlier. Scholes and Kellogg, writing in the mid-1960s, called attention to the divergence of plot and character. They pointed out that novelists from Henry Fielding to Leo Tolstoy have resisted this tendency, which has its roots in the substitution of psychology for myth. Nevertheless, in their words, "Serious works, in which the empirical is emphasized, get the characters; adventure stories get the plots."[11] A suggested example of this division is the distinction Graham Greene made between his "novels" and his "entertainments." Since the mid-1960s, it is apparent that the divergence has grown into a dichotomy, any possible pejorative connotation has been removed from the "entertainment" side, and a reintegration may have begun in Mexico. It would be impossible to deal with every suggestion of such a development. I will describe two cases in some detail: one novel, *La princesa del Palacio de Hierro*, by Gustavo Sainz; another, *Puerta del cielo*, by Ignacio Solares.

Sainz' first novel, *Gazapo* (1965), is about people in Mexico City whom my children, at that time, would have referred to as "kids" (meaning young adults who behaved as children occasionally). It is a novel of *la onda* — the "in" thing. Interesting characters very quickly become apparent; fresh and humorously appropriate language is immediately attractive. The novel is technically innovative, and some readers have been put off by the repetition, in various forms, of a very simple story. Nevertheless, *Gazapo*'s immediate attractions provided enough interest for a large public in spite of some reaction against its technique.

His second novel, *Obsesivos días circulares* (1969), in spite of being very carefully made, attracted far fewer readers. It does have story, and also character study, but they are cloaked in diversions and grotesqueries that lead many readers hopelessly astray. The novel's narrator-protagonist has trouble "getting it all together," to use the words of his contemporaries in the United States. His characterization is a fine commentary on a social circumstance, but it could not honestly be called easily accessible.

Sainz realized that *Obsesivos días circulares* had somehow failed to meet his goal as a novelist. The nature of this goal became amply apparent when, in the fall of 1974, he was interviewed repeatedly in connection with the publication of his third novel, *La princesa del Palacio de Hierro*. Basically, he believes that a novel should alter its readers' habits of perception. In order to accomplish this, Sainz the novelist attempts to create recognizable characters, invent unusual but believable happenings, and shake up his readers — to give them butterflies in the stomach.[12]

With *La princesa*, Sainz took no avoidable chances. Knowing well that Mexican publishers are not famous for imaginative advertising, he organized and carried out a campaign to attract readers. Beyond that, the book had to stand on its own. It is immediately attractive because Sainz again showed off his amazing sensitivity to the spoken language. However, analysis reveals several characteristics that might turn out to be negatives for some readers. The novel is a 300-page monolog that represents one side of a telephone conversation. The speaker is a woman in her thirties who recalls the adventures of her youth. She was a department store model, but her activities covered a rather wider range than modeling. We never know to whom she is talking. The narrator's position is not perfectly consistent. The ordering of events reflects the princesa's personality more accurately than it responds to the reader's sense of chronology. There are extraneous passages that may well be puzzling.

Why, then, is it that *La princesa del Palacio de Hierro* is a more accessible novel than *Obsesivos días circulares*? Stated very simply, Sainz has been careful to make one level of experience easy to appreciate, even while making other levels available to those who wish to achieve them. Karen J. Hardy has explained this procedure quite clearly in her study of the book.[13] She defines the first level of experience as focusing on the narrator-protagonist and the validity of her perception of her own experience. Beyond that, Hardy defines three other levels, or readings, and analyzes each. It is important for our purpose here to note a distinction claimed by Hardy for the Sainz novel. She says that, like many other contemporary novels, it "reveals new levels of meaning on each successive encounter or reading"; on the other hand, it is different because "it does not *demand* repeated readings before making accessible a complete experience."

The second case is *Puerta del cielo*, a first novel by Ignacio Solares, published in 1976. The story is perfectly clear and the people recognizable. A narrator using the third person tells the story of a middle-class Mexican youth who has to leave school and take a job in order to bolster the family economy. His experiences at work and in his first love affair combine to form his exterior reality. In addition, there are episodes narrated in the first person, in which the protagonist sees and talks with the Holy Virgin. It is interesting to note at least three characteristics of the novel that would have been commented on extensively in an earlier period: (1) the shift of narrative voice; (2) the appearance of the Virgin in absolutely commonplace, noncontemplative circumstances; and (3) the anomalous plot situation, which is both trite and inspired. Today, Solares' novel does not seem vanguardist at all. Indeed, it might be called traditionalist, although it obviously is not if we associate traditionalism with nineteenth-century realism.

Let us consider the opinion of *Puerta del cielo* expressed by Salvador Elizondo, high priest of hermeticism in Mexican fiction:

> This novel by Ignacio Solares bursts forth like the sun at midnight, in the panorama of recent fiction. . . . It comes, I believe, as a prudent corrective to the excesses of a well documented but opaque type of narrative. . . . At a time when almost all novels are written excessively, [this] one has neither too much nor too little.[14]

Going back to the first part of this essay, we now refer to four characteristics of Mexican fiction during the 1970s: (1) technical virtuosity and specialized allusions, (2) the author's fascination with observing the act of creating fiction, (3) complete metafiction (unless this characteristic be subsumed under number 2), and (4) a movement toward easier accessibility for more readers. These are characteristics, not categories. They do not indicate subperiods of the decade, although there may be some barely discernible process in their variation. Finally, if the fourth characteristic seems reactionary, it is so only in terms of the other three. It does not signal a return to the past.[15]

NOTES

1. Fell's paper, "Destrucción y poesía en la novela latinoamericana contemporánea," was presented at the Third Latin American Writers Conference, Caracas, July 1970. The paper was published in a volume entitled *III Congreso Latinoamericano de Escritores* (Caracas: Ediciones del Congreso de la República, 1971), pp. 207–213. The particular reference is to page 208, where the characteristic is described as "la fascinación frente a la creación creándose (como en *El hipogeo secreto* de Salvador Elizondo)."

2. Erich Auerbach, *Mimesis* (1946; reprint, Princeton, N.J.: Princeton University Press, 1968).

3. Ibid., p. 551.

4. The difference between rejection of new techniques and concern created by an unwelcome perception of reality might be explored profitably by reference to Roland Barthes' *Writing Degree Zero*. His definition of and references to *écriture* (modes of writing) create an interesting shift in the appearance of fiction's relationship to history. In addition, his discussion is relevant to what readers expect in a novel. The plurality and the meaning of *écriture* became concerns around 1850, a date associated with Gustave Flaubert and with the beginning of the decline of the bourgeoisie. It is interesting that Auerbach, when he points out the difficulty experienced by Joycean novelists in comprehending a fragmented reality, confesses that Flaubert was already having problems of this kind. For Barthes' views, see *Writing Degree Zero*, in a volume with his *Elements of Semiology* (Boston: Beacon Press, 1970), especially pp. 1–18, 29–40, 55–61.

5. Robert Scholes and Robert Kellogg, *The Nature of Narrative* (1968; reprint, London: Oxford University Press, 1975), p. 241. The point here is made as an illustration of the "ineluctable irony" of a narrative situation. The authors go on to say that "our pleasure in narrative literature . . . can be seen as a function of disparity of viewpoint or irony." The point I am making is closely related, although I am not inclined to discuss irony. It is quite apparent, within the Scholes and Kellogg formulation, that insofar as the reader participates as narrator, his relationship to the "disparity of viewpoint" changes, and so does his experience of the work.

6. Héctor Manjarrez, *Lapsus* (Mexico City: Joaquín Mortiz, 1971), pp. 21–22. Translation mine.

7. Pere Gimferrer, "El mapa y la máscara," *Plural* 5, no. 10 (julio 1976), 58–60. The specific reference is near the end of the third column on p. 58.

8. The narrator-reader relationship is extremely complicated. One way of illustrating my point is to use Roman Jakobson's model of a communication act. It may be found in his essay entitled "Linguistics and Poetics," published in *Style and Language*, edited by Thomas A. Sebeok (Cambridge, Mass.: MIT Press, 1960) and reprinted in *The Structuralists From Marx to Lévi-Straus*, edited by Richard and Fernande DeGeorge (Garden City, N.J.: Anchor Books, 1972). It takes this form:

Substituting appropriately and adding a step, I suggest the following:

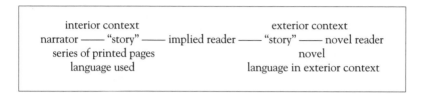

In this formulation, the communication act enclosed within the rectangle, taken as a whole, becomes the addresser who redirects the "story" to any one of millions of readers. The novel, now an object, is a fait accompli; but the communication act is not a fait accompli. The "story" remains the same insofar as the changed context and code will allow. However, if novel readers act as narrators, they must necessarily be in an equivocal position because there are actually two narrator positions in the model — one (within the rectangle) in which the novel readers would address the implied readers, and another (in place of the rectangle) in which the novel readers would address themselves. It seems that any creative satisfaction novel readers might enjoy by being thrust into the narrator position would be negated by the uncertain nature of their new role and by the ultimate sterility of talking to themselves.

Many studies are relevant to this problem. The two most helpful on the particular point I am making are John R. Searle, *Speech Acts* (London: Cambridge University Press, 1969), and Winifred Bryan Homer, *Text Act Theory: A Study of Nonfiction Texts* (Ph.D. dissertation, University of Michigan, 1975).

9. I have mentioned this phenomenon in another context: "Literary Periods in Twentieth-Century Mexico: The Transformation of Reality," in *Contemporary Mexico*, edited by James W. Wilkie, Michael C. Meyer, and Edna Monzón de Wilkie (Los Angeles: UCLA Latin American Center, 1976).

10. Robert Scholes, *Structuralism in Literature* (New Haven: Yale University Press, 1974), pp. 180–190.

11. Scholes and Kellogg, *The Nature of Narrative*, p. 237.

12. See, for example, Margarita García Flores, "Los secretos de una princesa," *La Onda*, supplement to *Novedades*, no. 71 (20 October 1974), pp. 6–7.

13. Karen J. Hardy, "Gustavo Sainz's *La princesa del Palacio de Hierro*: A Three-Hundred-Page Telephone Conversation," *Revista de Estudios Hispánicos* 13 (2) (1979), pp. 183–200.

14. Inside the cover (front and back) of Ignacio Solares, *Puerta del cielo* (Mexico City: Grijalbo, 1976).

15. This paper was originally published, in a slightly different form, under the title "Mexican Fiction in the Seventies: Author, Intellect, and Public," in *Ibero-American Letters in a Comparative Perspective*, edited by Wolodymyr T. Zyla and Wendell M. Aycock (Lubbock: Texas Tech Press, 1978).

Recent Mexican Fiction

FEDERICO PATÁN, *National University of Mexico (UNAM)*

In the past fifteen years or so, Mexican fiction has been following a pattern not too dissimilar from that of other countries: it has been expanding and deepening. But — and it was easy to predict — deepening and expanding according to its own spirit. Because of that, you could well ask: deepening how and expanding to where? Or even: deepening and expanding with what purpose? Trying to give an answer to these questions has kept literary critics quite busy recently. There is no month without its heavy quota of novels; some even sell handsomely, proof of which are the latest books by Héctor Aguilar Camín, Angeles Mastretta, and Laura Esquivel. Nowadays, keeping abreast of Mexican fiction means a relentless schedule of reading, note taking, and writing reviews.

If this general view of Mexican fiction is faithful — and I think it is — then the field is teeming with possibilities. Some of them are going to be the very essence of this essay. As the Mexican critic Evodio Escalante wrote not so long ago, "we are facing a conflictive, diversified, heterogeneous field" (p. 9), and the mere idea of pursuing the totality is just a dream. The late English critic Ann Duncan said more or less the same in 1983: "There would seem to be no clearly definable movements or trends in Mexican Literature today (perhaps attesting to its creative impetus and spontaneity)" (p. 117). One of the preeminent voices in this field, John S. Brushwood, has maintained that the years 1967 to 1982 were "a very complex period because of the variety of literary trends, the amount of new writers and the relative fecundity of publishing houses" (p. 14).

These are a variety of trends and a large number of writers, then. My purpose here is to attempt to bring a semblance of order into this ceaselessly growing field of activity. Of course, I am going to simplify a bit, just a bit, for the sake of clarity. So, my first general point is quite easy to make: Mexican fiction has been moving toward what Escalante calls "intellectual imagination," meaning a novel not directly concerned with a stark realism. The first fifty years of this century in Mexico belong to that unsophisticated way of writing known as realism, not having more exceptions than the literature of the group called Los Contemporáneos or the books of the Stridentist movement.

In the late 1940s and the beginning of the 1950s an important change comes about in Mexican fiction. Agustín Yáñez makes a name for himself with *Al filo del agua* (*The Edge of the Storm*, 1947), a complex novel where the already vanishing theme of the Mexican Revolution is discussed from a new, very modern, point of view: the characters are given a psychological depth never seen before in books of this type. Yáñez himself is very clear about it: "I wanted to write a novel, and this is the way the first four chapters were written, the four insomniacs, the four characters, with the atmosphere of the town as their only point of connection. . . . Once the characters, who are sleepless that particular night, were described, I wanted to connect them somehow, and I thought about a person who, that very same night, could be thinking about them: and this is the way the priest came to be . . ." (Carballo, p. 371). Yáñez adds that his intention was to use with a small town the narrative technique John Dos Passos applied to Manhattan. The old and pervasive way of considering reality as an unbreakable time continuum was no longer compulsory for a Mexican writer.

José Revueltas cuts an interesting figure here, because he also participates in changing the reality of Mexican fiction. He begins by going to the country — in *El luto humano* (*Human Mourning*, 1943) — but, once there, he gives his characters a human condition seldom seen before in Mexican literature. With Revueltas, the characters suddenly remember their psychology, and the dark side of men works on these people from the interior. As Carballo says, "the result is an acid literature (beautifully acid but, at the same time, horrible to feel) built up with the most sordid materials and, precisely because of that, the most authentic from the point of view of daily life" (Varios, p. 10). Almost immediately, and without giving up his world view, Revueltas moves gradually from the country to the city, being then one of the heralds of the already imminent urban fiction. Part of Revueltas' sense of reality is the way he accepts "the multiple approach school of Faulkner" (Varios, p. 16).

Juan Rulfo must be mentioned, of course. *Pedro Páramo* (1955) proves country people are not just working machines, ready to participate in any novel pertaining to social criticism. As did Revueltas, Rulfo knows that deep inside the distant look of peasants resides a mythical, magic, ancient, and wise, but also harsh, desolate, and black, view of the world. He goes for it, and succeeds in recreating such a world. And yet he does not forget how the terrible figure of Páramo, the *cacique*, imposes a heavy quota of cruelty on people.

And so we come to Carlos Fuentes. With him, we enter the urban world. *La región más transparente* (*Where the Air is Clear*, 1958) has the capital city as protagonist. To express the many-faceted reality of such a subject, Fuentes takes several devices from foreign literature and, as he says, these belong "mainly to Faulkner, Dos Passos, Lawrence and Huxley: the four great influences that I consciously admitted in the writing of the novel" (Carballo, p. 541). Lawrence, of course, is the writer capable of "reaching to the bottom of certain dark halves, certain nights of the spirit, certain muddy sediments of man" (Carballo, p. 542). Is it necessary to say that all of this becomes Mexico and only Mexico in Fuentes?

And so the future is ready: a diversified literature is opening for those coming after Yáñez, Revueltas, Rulfo, and Fuentes. The old realism is still alive and healthy for a few who keep caring for it, but now with the undiminishing presence of richer possibilities. And then, of course, *la onda*, a very irreverent way of measuring the adult world, and a very irreverent way of using — and sometimes misusing — the language of teenagers. The roads back to simplicity were closing.

This is the literary world inherited by new generations. They were smart: they took advantage, they learned, they explored, they are creating new ways, even though many of the participants are mistaken in seeing themselves as talented writers. They shall end as a necessary fertile soil for the real fiction.

And so, what about Mexican fiction today? Fuentes and *la onda* were discovering for us the many new facets of city life. And for a long while it seemed our literary geography was confined to the capital city, except for a few writers, Sergio Galindo one of the most relevant. But the rest of the country was patiently waiting for its moment. And this moment came in recent times, when a rather large group of fiction writers went back to their places of origin. With an acute sense of local atmosphere and language, they wrote about people in a specific region, though not forgetting that local color must have universal value — in other words, avoiding the dangerous ground of the picturesque. As Vicente Francisco Torres has emphasized, the always conflictful northern frontier of Mexico is a central focus of an important literary production. Jesús Gardea, Daniel Sada, Federico Campbell, and Ricardo Elizondo Elizondo are exploring with careful prose the confines of that region.

Next to the north, the region of Veracruz is one of the most prolific regions in Mexico when it comes to narrative. Galindo was already mentioned, but we must add Luis Arturo Ramos among the really important voices of today, as well as the lesser figure of Jaime Turrent. Herminio Martínez is drawing the history and present times of his home region, Guanajuato, and a very promising young writer, Severino Salazar, is doing the same with Zacatecas. Hernán Lara Zavala tells us about Yucatán, and a very prolific Rafael Ramírez Heredia goes once in a while to his side of the country, Tamaulipas.

This search for roots in parts of Mexico is to be commended. First of all, it balances the exceedingly strong presence of the capital city; then, it gives our literary map different colors and sounds. The small but important affairs of each region find a voice — and most of the time, a voice with the gift of the written word, because we are talking of novelists having the know-how. For example, Gardea, whose first book, *Los viernes de Lautaro*, appeared in 1979, has been exploring Placeres. Placeres is the name chosen to mask a real city: Delicias, in Chihuahua. Taking Faulkner's idea of Yoknapatawpha County as a model, Gardea tells about a way of living ruled by a deceivingly easygoing indifference, under which any passion is possible. Sada works language to the limit, trying to create a world where by no means is it easy to tell good from evil and where characters seldom come to be what they want to be. Campbell "turns power into the subject matter of a graphological, political and moral scrutiny" (Domínguez, p. 484). Elizondo Elizondo is very much under the shadow of the Colombian Gabriel García Márquez, but even so, he is a powerful writer.

One of the issues here concerns realism. As I said before, Mexican novel writing has been moving toward what Escalante calls "intellectual imagination," meaning a way of creation not directly interested in a stark realism. On the contrary, we have an increasing number of novelists prone to experiment with form, and rather careful in their use of colloquial language. So, when we come to the extreme naturalism of Rafael Gaona, Salvador Castañeda, Raúl Rodríguez Cetina, and even Armando Ramírez, their work seems too denotative, in all senses, if contrasted with the rich textures of Manuel Echeverría, Ignacio Solares, or María Luisa Puga. There is a real interest now in leaving behind the *onda* type of narration to search for a far more complex road to exposing reality to readers.

Because of this, metafiction has been a sort of obsession with Mexican writers during the last ten or twelve years. They use discourse to explore discourse, to discuss it in the process of constructing the novel. It has, to be sure, many ways of being present. For example, the novelist is part of the novel. As a character in the story, she informs the reader of the troubles she is having in writing the book the reader is reading. Of course, I am talking about *La forma del silencio* (1987) by Puga. Or you come to section six of *Ahora que me acuerdo* (1985), where Agustín Ramos says, "the backbone of this chapter will be the relationship between Margarita and Number One", and then gives some notes for the future composition of the text. Or we come, in *Antes* (1989), by Carmen Boullosa, to a narrative voice addressing the reader on matters of style by saying, for instance, "a while ago, when I was describing for you the world of my dreams, I said *the disorder which inhabited savagely the world of my dreams.* Why did I use the word savage? I could have said hasty, violent or sad . . ." Or you can even have a book — *Muchacho en llamas* (1988) by Gustavo Sainz — describing how another book by the same author — *Gazapo* (1965) — was written some twenty years before, giving, so to speak, two narrative lines on the same material. And we could go on adding titles to the list: *Los peligros del cristal* (1990), by Ana María Maqueo, *La insólita historia de la Santa de Cabora* (1990), by Brianda Domecq.

There is no doubt that the main purpose of this literary device is to adjust the relationship among writer, fictional world, and reader, and not to accept as the only possible link the idea that the novelized universe is for real, although the reader may know perfectly well that the writer is faking that reality. These novels seem to propose a new deal: reading with the full knowledge that the narrative universe is completely true only as a fictional entity, where a re-creation of external life is the valid concept — in other words, to be aware that the value of art depends on how well it gives an approach to life, with the emphasis going to *an*.

This tendency of Mexican fiction signifies, I surmise, that the unshakable certitude of nineteenth-century novels is no longer possible. Literature is reflecting the turmoil of modern society and, especially, the relative nature of all thinking about existence. Another trend among Mexican writers seems to be proving this: fragmentation of the *histoire* — no longer the consecutive telling of a certain plot, not even the mixing of time sequences, but the piecing of the events told, sometimes with the absence of some important fragments. You have it as a still tentative proposition in *Manifestación de silencios* (1987), by Arturo Azuela, a book in which the destruction of the capital city is reflected in the piecemeal nature of the text. You have it in *Síndrome de naufragios* (1984), by Margo Glantz, a putting together of the scattered remnants of a plot, the telling of a personal story mixed with the lives of some historical figures. You have it even more in Boullosa's *Mejor desaparece* (1987), a rather obvious title, where the adding up of fragments represents the difficult task of grasping the true meaning of reality. The utmost example is *Hemos perdido el reino* (1987), by Marco Antonio Campos, a novel consisting of 127 numbered fragments, each of them self-contained but, at the same time, part of the total view given by the book. The novel is about the earthquakes of 1985, and all the 127 pieces were taken from the newspapers, the TV news, or interviews with real people, so you have here a work of fiction whose subject matter comes almost verbatim from reality.

If I am not misreading these novels, they are saying that we live in a deteriorating world, and they are saying it by means of the stories told and the forms chosen to tell them. At the same time, at a higher level of abstraction, they are expressing the relative nature of the universe. Listen to the way Enrique López Aguilar (1991) presents such an idea: "The contemporary writer has just one possibility: that of looking into the world and explaining it in a fragmentary way or, even better, of fully doubting it, as the role of the artist is to offer questions, and not explanations" (p. 85).

The solid reality enjoyed in the past is no longer possible, and one must take into account the many ways a single event can be depicted. Most of the novels written nowadays touch on this matter, although not with the same degree of presence. Among the clearer examples we have a splendid — the best — book by Sergio Pitol: *El desfile del amor* (1984), a title whose two cultural referents are Ernest Lubitsch's 1929 film of the same name and the medieval dances of death. According to the plot, a historian comes back to Mexico after a long sojourn. His idea, almost an obsession, is trying to solve a murder committed forty years before, when he was a child. At the end of the investigation he has as many possible solutions as remaining witnesses. That is to say, he has no solution, and *that* is precisely one of the meanings of the book.

In a novel closer to a political reading of reality, *Morir en el golfo* (1986), Héctor Aguilar Camín, an important figure in the Mexican cultural world, is saying practically the same thing. When you try to reach the very center of the political mind ruling the country, what you find is one turn of the screw after another and, at the end of such a hazardous road, the sheer amount of information collected is a mass of contradictions masking the truth.

Let us go to a third example: Luis Arturo Ramos' *Este era un gato* (1987). Here, the different views of a single historical event are the result of the working of time. With a gap of nearly sixty years between the American invasion of Veracruz and the narrative present of the novel, a few old characters look at the personal history of one of the protagonists, Roger Copeland, going back to the past in search of clues to explain whatever may have happened then. Some young people, born after the event, try to get at the meaning of everything, but without the personal experience of that important past. As can be easily predicted, the result is a multiplicity of views.

A final example: *Dos voces*, co-written by Ana María Maqueo and Juan Coronado (1989) — a charming book, with a nice sense of humor and a playful approach to form. A divorced couple writes about their marriage. Maqueo is in charge of the female voice and Coronado of the male one. The novel goes to a narrative past in the sense of being epistolary, with chapter headings imitating those of a nineteenth-century novel. The male protagonist is not only co-writer of the material but also editor of all the documents, which he then sends to his ex-wife for comment. And she does comment, in a rather harsh epilog. We have here opposing points of view concerning almost everything. It was to be expected. And, of course, it is up to the reader to take one side of the issue, to accept the other, or to remain in a middle and neutral zone, wondering.

So Mexican fiction is exploring ways of expressing a conflictful reality, as if imprisoned in a sort of incertitude. And perhaps because of this, another important trend is present in our literature: history, and I do not mean just ancient history, but also events of twenty, thirty, or forty years ago. History is, and why not, a place where security can be found and, therefore, a way of removing the sense of danger. Two of the novels already mentioned — Pitol's and Ramos'— illustrate this tendency. And here, a necessary though perhaps obvious note: no single relevant novel written nowadays in Mexico fits into one category, thus testifying to the complex nature of this fiction.

The growing presence of history in a good number of Mexican novels seems to sum up what I have been describing: the search for a sort of stronghold, where the past may give us haven. It is, at the same time, the perfect place to look for the origins of our present condition. Here, some straight historical novels make the point clearly. *Gonzalo Guerrero* (1981), by Eugenio Aguirre, and *Juan Cabezón* (1985) and *Memorias del Nuevo Mundo* (1988), both by Homero Aridjis, explore carefully the cultural roots of Mexico, establishing the mixed condition of our nature. We have an ironic view of the near past in *Noticias del imperio* (1987), by Fernando del Paso, and we have the use of recent events in *El desfile del amor, Este era un gato,* and Luis Arturo Ramos' *Intramuros.* A curious case is that of Mario Huacuja's *La resurrección de la Santa María* (1989), in which a replica of Columbus' ship, built in 1988, gives voice to the spirit of the original vessel, allowing also the conclusion of Columbus' old dream: getting to Japan by sailing west.

And now, another sort of immersion in history: when the historical element is just a pretext to explore the most hidden clues of our existence as human beings. We have the mythical period described by Angelina Muñiz in *La guerra del unicornio* (1983), a clear allegory of the Spanish civil war, but also of any war where good and evil may be fighting for the soul of men. When Alberto Ruy Sánchez describes, in *Los demonios de la lengua* (1987), the misadventures of an eighteenth-century monk, he comes to the conclusion that the preaching of good ends by creating evil or (another possible interpretation) from the preaching of evil some good may come. The book closes with the following words: "A Saint lies here who did wrong and did it well." So, as we can see, we are dealing with a group of novels rather reluctant to give definite views of the world.

And now *El gringo viejo* (*The Old Gringo,* 1985). In this rather complex novel Carlos Fuentes goes back to a very concrete period of Mexican history, introduces enough data to re-create that particular moment, and then does away with history. By this we mean something very simple: the world external to the hacienda has no importance for a while, because the characters are living in a sort of timeless time where they explore their inner beings, the presence of others, the otherness of those presences. The author transforms the historical space into a mythical space and then, when the mutual exploration of the characters is done, gives back to history its original and predictable role. Of course, the general meaning goes far beyond the characters and touches more general cultural relationships.

Going into history can be assessed as a kind of exile, as a way of allowing ourselves a certain quota of nostalgia. Nostalgia and exile are two elements impossible to ignore in the latest Mexican fiction. They can be seen together in *El desfile del amor*, because the main character has just come back from abroad and is trying to find in the present the city he knew years before. In José Agustín's *Ciudades desiertas* (1983), *Dos voces*, and *Las aventuras de Euforión* (1988), by Roberto Vallarino, the characters, all of them Mexican, come face to face with a foreign culture while traveling, and then have to determine what to do about it. As is to be expected, trying to untangle the otherness of the world allows these persons to understand themselves better. Another characteristic that all of these authors share is a sharp sense of irony, usually to be found in books about other countries: just remember Mark Twain.

The opposite image is present in another group of novels in which somebody comes to Mexico from another country and, therefore, culture. *The Old Gringo* is again a work to be mentioned here, but also Arturo Azuela's *El don de la palabra* (1984), about a Spanish exile in Mexico; *Las hojas muertas* (1987), by Bárbara Jacobs, a tender exploration of a paternal image through the eyes of three daughters, the father being a foreigner; *La "flor de lis"* (1987), by Elena Poniatowska, where the strange reality of Mexico is seen through the wondering eyes of a very young girl; and *Ultimo exilio* (1986), by Federico Patán, where a foreign gaze regards the strange ways of Mexico and wonders first, tries to understand later, and ends by living Mexico as a sort of very complex enigma.

In describing recent Mexican fiction, I have been using words such as "metafiction" and "fragmentation" concerning form; a variety of focuses, the use of history, and the presence of otherness in the plots. All of this points to a very definite conclusion: Mexican fiction is quite aware of the shaky condition of its society; at the same time, it is quite aware of the need to reflect that shaky condition. Awareness is present in knowing that a single event has many explanations. Precisely because of this, my exposition is one of the many readings Mexican narrative allows. A different critic, with the same selection of books, could — would — give another view, equally valid or equally debatable. And with a different choice of novels. . . . So, back we are with Ann Duncan: this condition is the best proof that Mexican literature is living an important moment.

REFERENCES

Brushwood, John S. 1985. *La novela mexicana 1967–1982*. Mexico City: Grijalbo.

Carballo, Emmanuel 1986. *Protagonistas de la literatura mexicana*. Segunda Serie de Lecturas Mexicanas, 48. Mexico City: El Ermitaño/SEP.

Duncan, Ann 1983. "Innovations in Mexican Prose Fiction since 1970. *Hispanic Journal* (Pennsylvania), 1 (Fall): 117–127.

Escalante, Evodio. 1988. *La intervención literaria*. Mexico City: Universidad Autónoma de Sinaloa/Universidad Autónoma de Zacatecas.

López Aguilar, Enrique. 1991. *La mirada en la voz*. Mexico City: Universidad Autónoma de Tlaxcala/Universidad Autónoma de Puebla.

Varios. 1984. *Revueltas en la mira*. Mexico City: Universidad Autónoma Metropolitana.

Desire and the Frontier: Apparitions from the Unconscious in *The Old Gringo*

DAVÍD CARRASCO, *University of Colorado at Boulder*

> She was there. In the middle of the crowd, struggling and pushing and trying to find her place, gazing at the faces that blurred into one, wanting to be a witness to the spectacle. From the middle of the silent throng of sombreros and rebozos emerged those gray eyes fighting to retain a sense of their own identity, of personal dignity and courage in the midst of a vertiginous terror of the unexpected. (p. 33)

This description of Harriet Winslow, the Anglo-American who has come to Mexico to instruct Mexican children "in the English tongue" (p. 34), appears immediately after a description of hanged men on telephone poles and reflects one of the major themes of Carlos Fuentes' novel, *The Old Gringo:* the fluidity, instability, and even illegitimacy of social place and personal self in revolutionary Mexico. Consciousness roves while buildings, bridges, and bodies burn. Even the terror is vertiginous, whirling.

There is more to this theme, for the protagonist is not just out of place with her Gibson Girl look in the Chihuahua desert and her sense of identity fading; she is also exercising a crucial act of survival by "gazing at the faces that blurred into one" (p. 33). She struggles to see, to "be a witness to the spectacle" (p. 33) and gain some angle of orientation within it. Consider the passage that precedes this description to appreciate what she is facing:

> A whistling sound settled over everything as the old gringo stared with atavistic horror at the row of hanged men strung on the telegraph poles,

---

Unless otherwise specified, all quoted material in this chapter is taken from *The Old Gringo* by Carlos Fuentes, translated by Margaret Sayers Peden. New York: Farrar, Straus & Giroux, 1985. Used with permission of the author.

mouths agape, tongues protruding. They were all whistling, swinging in the soft desert breeze, all along the avenue leading to the burning hacienda. (p. 32)

Both Harriet and the old gringo have come to Mexico seeking new selves (he a dead one, she a living one) and see a whirling terror and an archaic horror. They learn that they carry these and other spectacles within their own lives and are forced to cope by performing unwanted acts of self-awareness. These acts show the reader that in Fuentes' view, the line of sight that leads to insights is not primarily visual but visionary, a line of sight streaming through dreams, repressed memories, psychological transferences and associations. Each awareness is tinctured with religious imagery approaching apparition. These apparitions are born not from heaven but from the unconscious mind of each major protagonist.[1] The old gringo sees and is seen as "God the Father" (p. 55), whereas Harriet has a dark vision, which is both history and fantasy, of a female seductress in the underworld, and General Tomas Arroyo transforms his raped mother into a virginal fantasy. In each case, the image is actually visualized and involves the desire for a deceased father or mother.

Fuentes manages this fluidity between surface and depth by employing the core metaphor of the frontier and of crossing the frontier throughout the novel. He achieves focus in the metastatic world of the Mexican Revolution by creating a series of theatrical stage sets on which spectacles of border crossings between outer and inner, childhood and adulthood, history and imagination take place. Some of the bridges linking these different types of spaces are psychological transferences that displace powerful feelings and sexual wishes experienced at earlier stages in life onto a contemporary person or situation. As we shall see, these stage sets consist of male spaces, even patriarchal spaces, such as the hacienda, the railroad car, the battlefield, the "Second Empire mansion" (p. 49) where fathers have sex with forbidden women, rape, kill, are killed, or wish to be killed. In what follows I will interpret a series of border crossings, relations between surface and interior spectacles, through two readings of The Old Gringo: first a personal reading of amusement and recognition and second a more probing reflection on apparitions from the unconscious mind.

FIRST READING: AMUSEMENT AND RECOGNITION

An intriguing process of personal recognition unfolded during my first reading of the novel. I was so taken with the book (I even dreamed several new versions of selected passages) that I invented a small cascade of potential titles for an as-yet-to-be-written paper in order to control "the fever of perceptions" (p. 37) that move the characters through the landscapes of Washington, D.C.; El Paso; San Francisco; Chihuahua; and their dreams. I first thought of the title "A Frontier of Memories: Place and No Place in *The Old Gringo*" to reflect the structure of the novel that begins and ends (in the English version at least) with Harriet Winslow remembering, while sitting in Washington, D.C., her time in the Mexican Revolution when she crossed the sexual and dream frontiers that are scars in Mexican-American relations. This title was suggested by the exchange about the Miranda hacienda between the old gringo and Harriet when she insists,

" 'I intend to take charge of this place until the legitimate owners return. Would you do the same?' "
" 'There is no 'place.' It's burned to the ground' " (p. 41).

Reading further, I switched to "Carlos Fuentes and the Grateful Dead" to reflect the persistent, mocking attitudes toward death, how people die, how they look when they die, and the exhumation of the old gringo, who went to Mexico seeking death and who died twice (and was buried twice and in two countries), as did Tomas Arroyo, to represent the exhumation of primal scenes of sexual intercourse that are recovered in ecstatic moments of "love without loving" (p. 123).

I was rescued from this title when I came to one of the pivotal scenes in the flashy private railroad car moving through the tragic Chihuahua landscape when the revolutionary General Arroyo and the old gringo face off silently against each other over papers as brittle as old silk telling of the legitimate claim the peons have to the land. Reading, I thought — this book is not about writing or journalism or Ambrose Bierce but about reading, how Mexicans read the landscape with their memories and need "papers" whenever they get within twenty miles of any border, political or apocalyptic, how gringos read the books they have written that contain symbolic maps of the border landscape. "Reading and Memory in the *The Old Gringo*," I decided, but this title was replaced when the Mexicans entered the ruins of the Miranda ballroom with Versailles mirrors and saw their entire bodies reflected, for the first time in their lives, exclaiming, " 'Look, it's you. It's Me. It's Us' " (p. 40), as they become disturbed by the presence of their reflections. "When Mirrors Are Windows" became my title even when I saw how Fuentes made people mirrors of each other, mirrors into which they looked and saw their past heartbreaks, violations, dreams. But these mirrors became like certain Picasso images, refracted images of the "other" and childhood, when General Arroyo forcefully seduced Harriet Winslow and her body, evoking the soul dream that she is experiencing the embrace of the father who abandoned her, that she is at once herself and the colored woman of turn-of-the-century Washington her father possessed in a cellar. At the same time the general desires Harriet as much as he desired his mother to come back from the dead.

This title changed when I saw that this book is about how our dreams, which we dream while awake and asleep, are attached to our very bodies and the bodies we inhabited as children and adolescents, bodies which, when we enter them, are like dreams we are entering, gaining new access to and restoring life. "Bodies Which Are Dreams in Fuentes' Imagination," I thought.

Then, when I saw how desire and fire transform the novel, when fire guts the hacienda of oppression and men fire periodically at each other and sexual fires of searing heat become thresholds on the road to dream and the moon-faced woman tells how her vicious husband "decorated her cunt" (p. 152) with the Sacred Heart of Jesus and the old gringo provokes his own death by burning those precious papers, I thought of "The Symbolism of Fire and Fragmentation in The Old Gringo."

But this series of titles, in part a technique to summarize the book, must be juxtaposed with another title, sarcastically intended, that came to me from reading a newspaper item. "Misled by Jane Fonda" occurred to me when I read that Jane Fonda had decided to make the film The Old Gringo after she visited the excavation of the Great Aztec Temple in Mexico City several years ago. She said something like, "After I climbed down and saw the ancient roots of this culture hidden below the streets, I decided to make The Old Gringo." This irked me because I had worked at Templo Mayor and climbed down maybe thirty times and never once had seen a connection between the Aztec shrine and a movie about Chihuahua and the Mexican Revolution. This irked me because Raymond Williams, knowing my interest in cities and novels, had urged me to read *Where the Air is Clear* by Carlos Fuentes, which is about a "city ancient in light, . . . city in the true image of gigantic heaven," in preparation for the First Novel of the Americas Conference in 1989, and now I was misled by Jane Fonda to see what was so significant about a novel about gringos!

And then, as I entered *The Old Gringo*, I experienced what Fuentes has said about his *first* reading of Gabriel García Márquez' *One Hundred Years of Solitude* and the element of immediate recognition present in the book: "There is a joyous rediscovery of identity here, an instant reflex by which we are presented, in the genealogies of Macondo, to our grandmas, our sweethearts, our brothers and sisters, our nursemaids."[2] I misled myself because of a personal issue for me: a rediscovery of identity of my strange family's history, my grandparents and my father and mother. The novel is set in Chihuahua, the home of my paternal grandparents, who fled into El Paso, where the old gringo first appears, during the Mexican Revolution. But Harriet Winslow remembers it all from Washington, D.C., near where I grew up and played basketball with blacks along Rock Creek Park, where she walked and near where she spied on her father and the Negress in the D.C. summer. In fact, at one point, while reading descriptions of the luminous mist, dripping green roofs, and dank air in the nation's capital, I whiffed again those dead magnolias of the D.C. jungle I smelled as a boy. And my Chihuahua grandmother and her sisters were nannies in Anglo homes in Chihuahua (my father admitted, "They also did domestic work; we can't deny that") and traveled with them across the frontier into the United States; Harriet Winslow wanted to become a governess for the Mirandas and tried hard to domesticate the rebels' women and children in the Anglo style. My grandmother Carlota Carranza was in Parral the day Pancho Villa (Doroteo Arango) was assassinated, and Villa assassinates Tomas Arroyo in the novel. And my father played for the national Mexican basketball team in the Central American games in the late 1930s, the team from Chihuahua called the Dorados, the name of Villa's rebel forces. Finally it gets weird. My mother's father was a soldier in the First World War and was buried, like the old gringo, in a soldier's grave in Arlington National Cemetery; and if that isn't enough, his name was Ambrose — the first name of the old gringo, Ambrose Bierce! My father, who when he heard me read passages over the phone of the Mexicans talking about the old gringo's larger-than-life character, said, "I know that kind of talk about gringos," and then went out and bought the book so he could rediscover scenes of his adolescence, when he struggled to decide which side of the border he would live on; which citizenship, Tex-Mex or Chihuahuense, he would retain.

So my first reading of the novel led me back across the Mexican border into my family history and back across the border the other way into my family history, into genealogies of old gringos and old Mexicans.

SECOND READING:
CROSSING THE INNER FRONTIER

> "And the frontier in here?" the North American woman had asked, tapping her forehead. "And the frontier in here?" General Arroyo had responded, touching his heart. "There's one frontier we only dare to cross at night," the old gringo said. "The frontier of our differences with others, of our battles with ourselves." (p. 5)

The Old Gringo is a book of apparitions, spectres, and dreams.[3] At the start Harriet Winslow is visited by apparitions, and she "sees over and over the spectres of Tomas Arroyo and the moon-faced woman and the old gringo cross her window" (p. 3). These spectres cross the border between her past and her forever solitude, and she is reminded of another border she saw and was forbidden to cross. She remembers Tomas Arroyo showing her "what she could be and then forbidding her to ever be what she might be. And she knew she could never be that, and in spite of knowing it, he let her see it" (p. 3). Perhaps this denial was a sweet Mexican revenge against all gringos who "spent their lives crossing frontiers, theirs and those that belonged to others" (p. 5). As the passage above shows, these crossings are connected with frontier crossings in the head and heart that "we only dare to cross at night" (p. 5), in our dreams, or in the darkness, in private visions. For Fuentes, the real frontiers are interior, and they have two crucial dimensions of difference — the differences we have with others and the conflicts within ourselves.

This complexity and fluidity of the category of frontier in the novel appears in a macabre border crossing at the start, with the exhumation of the old gringo's body from his Chihuahua grave (as we later learn, so that it can be symbolically killed a second time). This physical exhumation leads to the exhumation of the entire story from Harriet Winslow's memory, and we learn that the old gringo came to Mexico to die because

" 'to be a gringo in Mexico . . . Ah, that is euthanasia. That's what the old gringo said' " (p. 9). To be a gringo in Mexico is to be either headed for or in the grave. But even that destiny of place is not secure, for the old gringo must be disinterred and reappear on earth, "where a group of soldiers for a few seconds held the pose of the Pietà" (p. 9) as they prepared him for shipment to Pancho Villa and then to Washington, D.C.

A Chasm of Consciousness

The first act of awareness involving inner frontiers occurs in the flashy railroad car when the old gringo and General Arroyo attempt to enter each other's minds and establish the superiority of their views of the revolution. The old gringo has been tentatively accepted into the revolutionary force as someone whose "eyes are filled with prayers" (p. 24) and whose hands are quick with a gun. This railroad car is the first patriarchal space of the novel. It is owned, run, and populated by men and is associated in the old gringo's mind with a space used to serve men.

> They were in the General's private car, which reminded the old gringo of the interior of one of the whorehouses he'd liked to visit in New Orleans. He sank into a deep red velvet armchair and sardonically stroked the tassels of the gold-lame curtains. The chandelier hanging precariously above their heads tinkled as the train began chugging down the track. Young General Arroyo tossed down his glass of mescal, and the old man, without a word, imitated him. (p. 26)

The two men begin to bicker and maneuver for position when the old gringo insults Arroyo by noting that "the General had been a peon on the Miranda hacienda and was now getting even riding around in the flashy private railroad car that once belonged to his master" (pp. 27–28). Arroyo blurts out, " 'You don't understand, gringo,' . . . in a thick and incredulous voice. 'You really don't understand. Our papers are older than theirs' " (p. 28). To prove his case about the revolution, he brings out old but precious land grant papers from the King of Spain protecting hard-working men and women against the *encomienda* system and its terrible exploitation. An intense confrontation of mind and heart takes place in which differences with others are a chasm. This is one frontier that won't be easily crossed.

Each has a radically different "manner of knowing . . . the story" (p. 28) of the history and meaning of the land. For the old gringo, legitimate access to political knowledge comes through books and journalism. For Arroyo this knowledge comes through memory and a handful of fragile papers he shows to his taunting adversary. Significantly, these powerful differences are not verbalized so much as imagined by the two in a clairvoyant exchange.

> The General and the gringo looked at each other in silence, communicating from opposite sides of a deep chasm; their looks were their words, and the land flowing past the train window behind each of them told the story of the papers, which was the story of Arroyo and also the history in the books, which was the story of the gringo. . . . He saw in Arroyo's eyes what Arroyo was telling him in different words, he saw in the passing Chihuahua landscape, in its tragic gesture of loss, less than Arroyo could tell him but more than he himself knew. As if the story kept flowing without interrupting the rhythm of the train, or the rhythm of Arroyo's memory . . . each watched the advances, the retreats, the movements in the eyes of the other. (pp. 28–29)

In the face of Arroyo's stronger position, the old gringo tries insult: " 'My dear General, you can read?' the gringo asked, a glinting smile in his gaze. The mescal was fiery stuff that stirred his worst instincts" (p. 30). To this affront, Arroyo blurts out,

> "You think that organ-pipe cactus can read and I can't? You are a fool, gringo. I may not be able to read, but I can remember.". . . Repeatedly, the General tapped his brow with his forefinger: all the stories, all the histories, are here in my head, a whole library of words; the history of my people, my village, our pain: here in my head. (p. 30)

Later, in a morbid gesture, the old gringo turns this knowledge about Arroyo's loyalties against himself.

The preciousness of these papers and the depth of their meaning are illustrated by reference to something even more potent in Arroyo's head. Fuentes introduces one of the most important lines of free association in the novel when we are told, "The Mexican stroked the papers as he would stroke his mother's cheek, or the curve of his lover's hip" (p. 29). Connections, powerful emotional connections among the revolution, the papers, sexual intercourse, and the desire for one's parents characterize the frontier of the unconscious to which we now turn.

NEGRESS IN THE UNDERWORLD,
VIRGIN ON THE DANCE FLOOR

The stream of consciousness linking revolution to sex and desire
for family reappears in the mixing of scenes acted out in two more
patriarchal spaces — the Mexican hacienda and the Anglo mansion in
Washington, D.C. In both places a female domestic "spectacle" dedicated to putting furniture and people in order is linked by a sexual
transference.[4] Domestic surfaces such as mirrors, tabletops, and lamps
stimulate the displaced sexual feelings and wishes of adolescence to
appear in the present.

In spite of its ruin, Harriet decides to civilize the hacienda, to be
"the instructress for a hacienda that no longer existed" (p. 38). After she
makes the acquaintance of the old gringo and they tentatively build an
emotional alliance against the Mexicans, they enter the Miranda ballroom, a miniature Versailles with mirrors ceiling to floor — "mirrors
destined to reproduce in a round of perpetual pleasure the elegant steps
and movements of couples from Chihuahua, El Paso and other hacien-
das, come to dance the waltz and the quadrille on the elegant parquet
Señor Miranda had brought from France" (p. 39).

Stimulated by reflections of her father in the old gringo, she blurts
out her unconscious reason for coming to Mexico: she is searching for
her lost father. " 'My father. He disappeared during the Spanish American War. The army lent him dignity, and us as well . . .' " (p. 38). The
narrative develops the previous hint of sexual transference found in
Arroyo's papers when Harriet remembers another domestic space and
another reflection on her mother's tabletop, which leads her back to
what psychoanalysis calls a primal scene of sexual desire:[5]

> Now she stared at the light in the center of her mother's favorite table, a
> marble-topped table her father had used every night for paperwork and
> the bills, and the family for eating, and now her mother used only for the
> latter. She stared at that domestic glow and realized that she had invested
> this simple household object, this everyday necessity, this green-shaded
> lamp with all the trembling imagination, all the passionate desire of the
> light she remembered from that humid summer mansion. (pp. 49–50)

Fuentes acknowledges that "this light worked the transference" (p. 50)
back to her dreams and her father. She "dreamed a lot" and "like a dream,

her soul revealed itself in flashes" (p. 48), and the flash that haunts her waking and sleeping life is another "brilliant yellow light" spied on as a girl "moving slowly from floor to floor in a recently constructed but already decaying mansion on Sixteenth Street" (p. 49). This light transforms the building into an erotic interior — "the light . . . slowly . . . came and went, melting what must have been the soft interior, the buttery recesses behind the facade of carved stone" (p. 49).

Harriet resists the force of the transference, in dreams and conversation, "the investment . . . of her trembling imagination" (pp. 48–49) working within her, but eventually she arrives where the light takes her, an underground place of smells, noises, and shadows. As a child, we discover, she had followed the light and her father into a cellar of the mansion, where she smelled something:

> First, the smell of old mattresses and damp rugs, and then the other half, the smell of the couple lying there, the sour sweet smell of love and blood, the moist armpits and genital spasms as her father possessed the solitary Negress who lived there, perhaps in the service of absent masters. (p. 50)

The dark woman in the underground utters phrases of desire: "Captain Winslow, I am very lonely. You may have me at your pleasure" (p. 51).

Harriet is uncovering, layer by layer in Mexico, a primal sexual scene. She recollects, after fierce resistance, the spectacle of her father and a forbidden woman engaging in sexual intercourse. Fuentes' language and imagery tint the memory with a religious meaning. She is in the underworld in the cellar, and undergoing — through multiple senses: hearing, smell, vision — an illumination that is traumatic and potentially damaging to her.

This primal scene comes more fully to disturb her, and us. It is as though we are the intense observers stimulating the narrative by our reading, as can be noted in two other scenes, which involve a shared dream and a dance. Harriet is sleeping in the railroad car when the old gringo enters and watches her. He lightly kisses her cheek. He crosses the frontier of her mind by divining her dreams and becomes implicated in them:

> Perhaps he wanted to invite her into his own dream; but his was a dream of death that could not be shared with anyone. However, as long as they both lived, no matter how great the distance between them, they could

penetrate each other's dreams, share those dreams. He made a tremen-
dous effort, as if they might be the last act of his life, and in an instant he
dreamed with open eyes and clenched lips Harriet's entire dream, everything; the missing father; the mother, a prisoner of shadows; the transfer
of the fixed light on the table and the fleeting light in the abandoned
house. (pp. 52–53)

In this clairvoyance, fueled by paternal sexual desire, it may be that he
hears the Negress whispering in her father's ear, "I am very lonely. You
may have me at your pleasure."

The complex connections between this "transfer of the fixed light
on the table and the fleeting light in the abandoned house" (p. 53) and
the primal-primordial sexual scene are completed later, when Harriet is
dancing in Arroyo's arms before the mirrors. She has failed to "civilize"
(p. 41) the Mexicans, and the rebels have returned victorious from a
battle. As their bodies heat up to each other, her senses reach back to
Washington, her father, and the cellar: "She was dancing the slow waltz
with him but also with her father: I am dancing with my father just back
from Cuba, decorated in Cuba, promoted in Cuba, saved by Cuba, savior
of Cuba" (p. 109). This grandiose father who went to Cuba to save it
parallels the grandiose daughter who came to "save Mexico" (p. 109).
She "would set the example; she would be the symbol around which all
the work of restoring the hacienda would revolve" (p. 93). But an
example of what kind of person or symbol? She is portrayed as follows:

Harriet dancing this night with her ramrod-straight, decorated brave
father . . . with stiff mustaches and hair smelling of cologne . . . and she
burying her nose in her father's neck, smelling the city of Washington
there, that false Acropolis of marble and omens and columns sunk in the
wet mud of a pernicious tropics that dared not say its name: a Southern
suffocation, a jungle of marble like a grandiose and empty cemetery, the
temples of justice and the government sinking into an equatorial, devour-
ing, spreading tangle of undergrowth; a vegetal cancer rooted in the
foundation of Washington, a city moist as the crotch of an aroused
Negress: Harriet buried her nose in Tomas Arroyo's neck and smelled a
Negress's swollen, velvety sex: Captain Winslow, I am very lonely, you
may have me at your pleasure. (pp. 109–110)

This luscious transference of a primal scene and a patriarchal space
to a revolutionary scene in Mexico displays a riotous dexterity of

consciousness. The Mexican general she previously despised but who is now seducing her becomes her "ramrod" father whose neck reminds her of the pernicious tropics of a city which reminds her of the crotch of an aroused Negress which associates Arroyo's neck and back with the velvety sex of her father's underground lover. The implications of how frontiers of consciousness are crossed are astonishing. In a fantastic reversal, the Mexican becomes a gringo father and the Anglo woman becomes the Negress having sex with her father. The Negress appears only as a voice and a vagina, never a face, in the novel.[6] Yet the stimulus she has had in Harriet's life is enormous.

Fuentes does not rest here. One psychological transference leads to another; in fact, crosses from one mind to the other. While Harriet is dancing with Arroyo/father, Arroyo presses close to her belly, becoming displaced in the imagination to his childhood and fantasizing a mother he never had. He thinks of Harriet's pubic hair, the

> tangled growth there as a beautiful forest he would always see from afar, and from behind a door of mirrors the boy Tomas Arroyo came out to dance with his mother, his mother, his father's legitimate wife, his mother, the straight and clean woman without a weight of clouds on her shoulders, without a crown of cold winds on her brow, without eyes ashen from the sun, but clean, no more than that . . . dancing with her son the waltz "Sobre las olas.". . . (p. 110)

After that, Tomas Arroyo "put his tongue in Harriet Winslow's ear" (p. 110).

We learn later that Arroyo is actually the illegitimate son of the tyrant *hacendado* Miranda, who raped Arroyo's mother and abandoned her. Thus, his name is actually Tomas Miranda. We learn at the end of the novel that his father was shot to death in Yucatan after having keys shoved down his throat for raping another beautiful Indian girl in another hacienda. The father was then hung up in public by his balls.

In this apparition of Arroyo's mother we see a religious sensibility reflecting the Virgin, or at least a "clean" mother. She is cleaned up in Arroyo's vision of her; she is upright, legitimate, and with a bright face. Yet he sticks his tongue in her ear! And thinks privately, mixing both mothers into one image and mixing that one image with Harriet Winslow, " 'I want you, more than you can imagine, little gringa. I'll tell you how much. I want you like I want my mother back again. That much.

Forgive me but I will do whatever I have to do to have you tonight, my beautiful gringa' " (p. 113).

OLD GRINGO'S GOD THE FATHER

"Nobody wants to see gringo soldiers in our land," stated Carlos Fuentes during an interview in the Mesoamerican Archive at the University of Colorado at Boulder in September 1989.

One concept that Fuentes explores not only in his novels but in his literary criticism is the "mythical and simultaneous novel," the novel that combines historicity and myth, fact and fantasy. This combination is not just a melting pot, a search for a new mix, but rather a search for the possibilities of freedom and liberation from the fatality of history. He writes in *Myself with Others* about his discoveries during the second reading of *One Hundred Years of Solitude*. This reading

> conflates, both factually and fantastically, the order of what has happened (the chronicle) and the order of what might have happened (the imagination), with the result that the fatality of the former is liberated by the desire of the latter. Each historical act of the Buendias in Macondo is a sort of axis around which whirl all the possibilities unbeknown to the external chronicler but which, notwithstanding, are as real as the dreams, the fears, the madness, the imagination of the [actor of his — or her story].[7] (p. 190)

The old gringo's attempt at liberation from the fatality of history through the desire of the imagination, is wildly presented in another patriarchal space, the battlefield. The old man charges through a *federale* brigade in the Chihuahua desert attacking the apparition of his Civil War father. This scene follows immediately upon the old gringo's clairvoyant penetration into Harriet's "entire dream" (p. 53). He has ridden with Arroyo and his men to battle the federal soldiers in the foothills. His mind contains "a terrible emptiness, almost an oblivion" (p. 54), and he fills this void with his desire to attack his father — a familiar desire, because as a younger man fighting in the Civil War, "he had wanted to fight on the side of the Blue, with the Union, against the Gray, the Rebels, simply because he had dreamed that his father was serving in the Army of the Confederacy, against Lincoln. He wanted what he had dreamed: the revolutionary drama of son against father" (p. 54). He disobeys Arroyo's order to dismount and observe the enemy and instead charges, machine-gun fire passing over his head. He becomes a fantastic apparition, a god even, a Don Quixote attacking not windmills but his father's ghost. As Arroyo's men fall flat on the ground out of range of the gunfire, the old gringo miraculously avoids becoming a fatality of history and is instead transformed into a fiery figment of everyone's imagination. The bullets miss him, and the enemy troops see

> the mirage of a white knight on a white horse, so visible he seemed invisible.... They saw him coming, but the truth was, they didn't believe it.... He wasn't like them, he was an avenging white devil, he had eyes that only God in the churches had, his Stetson flew off and they saw revealed the image of God the Father. He was in their imaginations: he wasn't real. (pp. 54–55)

But they aren't real either in the old gringo's mind, for he also desires and sees a devil, a god, his father behind them:

> The handful of Federal soldiers were so stunned by the vision that they were slow to recover their senses, clumsy in exchanging machine gun for rifles, never realizing that behind them a Confederate commander on horseback, his sword unsheathed, was urging them on to victory, and that it was toward this horseman, flashing his anger from the mountaintop, the gringo rode, not toward them, their machine gun lost now, lassoed and tumbled out of sight and then the wrinkled sere apparition fired on the four sharpshooters and they lay dead beneath the burning sun.... (p. 55)

The old gringo's senses are absorbed completely into this fantasy as the rebels yell in celebration at his achievement: "he did not hear it: he was still firing upward, toward the peaks where first rode, and then fell, the horseman dressed in gray, but whiter than he, hurtling through the air: the horseman in the sky" (pp. 55–56).

The simultaneous nature of the world in *The Old Gringo* represented here reveals another religious image, the image of God the Father. An actual skirmish in Chihuahua stimulates an obsessive fantasy of an imaginary battle in the Civil War, in which the old gringo becomes for an instant God the Father in the eyes of the *federales* and they become the forces protecting the god, the father, he hungers to murder.

HISTORY BENT OVER

The scene just described shows one of Fuentes' ways of dealing with and escaping from history, but in this case gringo history. Mexican history in the novel — the weight and fatality of Mexican history — appears in the next chapter, when Harriet Winslow insults General Arroyo by telling him he is not a general, not a true military man as her father was. In a rage, Arroyo pulls her outside and forces her to see and acknowledge the history of the "accursed land" (p. 61) where the Mirandas had vacationed, become bored, drunk cognac while the people breathed air "draped in mourning" (p. 63). The Mirandas

> fought the young bulls. They also went galloping through the tilled fields, terrifying the peons bent over their humble Chihuahua crops, beans, wild lettuce, spindly wheat; they beat the backs of the weakest men with the flat of a machete, and they lassoed the weakest women and raped them in the hacienda stables while the mothers of the young gentlemen pretended not to hear the screams of our mothers and the fathers of the young gentlemen drank cognac in the library and said, "They're young, this is the age of sowing their wild oats, better now than later. They'll settle down. We did the same." (p. 61)

What they had done in fact was rape a young girl, Arroyo's mother, and drive him and his kind into a crushing silence. How did this little bastard become a general; who named him general? He explains:

> "Misfortune named me general. Silence named me general, having to hold my tongue. Here they killed you if you made any noise in bed. If a man and a woman moaned while they were in bed together, they were whipped. That was lack of respect for the Mirandas. They were decent people. We made love and we gave birth without a sound, señorita. Instead of a voice, I have a paper." (p. 62)

He also has, as we have seen, a memory in his head in place of an alphabet or literacy.

CASTRATION AND SEXUAL COMBAT

Sounds, making love, and what people have in their heads and mouths are drawn together in the sexually climactic scene of the novel. In bed, Arroyo has disclosed that he came back to the Miranda hacienda to give his followers the "big gift" (p. 24) of seeing themselves in the mirrors, and that he is trapped there, where "he had been as if mesmerized for nearly thirty years, as a child, and a boy, and a young man of the hacienda" (p. 127). Now he is locked in again by the memory of a lesson about dignity and a gift of the box of papers given by Don Graciano, the servant and key keeper of the hacienda. Harriet discovers a searing heat in her attraction for Arroyo, and their sexual scene oscillates violently between moments of profound pleasure and pain. Finally it turns into a vicious spectacle of dominance and power in which she feels overwhelmed. One moment she comes

> with an unbearable groan, a great animal moan she would have tolerated in no one, a sinful sigh of pleasure that was God-defying, duty mocking (she would not have tolerated it in herself, a month ago), a scream of love that told the world that this was the only thing worth doing, worth having, worth knowing, nothing else in the world, nothing else but this instant between that other instant that gave us birth and that final instant that took our life away forever. (p. 196)

And the next moment of this spectacle she "violently wrenched herself from Arroyo's body with a gesture more fearful than castration" (p. 196). Then (or it could be earlier in Fuentes' simultaneous novel) their sex stimulates in her mind images of a bullfighter in a vacant ring at night, surrounded by the dead smell of carcass and the impulse for castration and murder. Harriet plunges into oral sex, and "she felt she could bite it off if she wished, and before he had been able to thrust like a sword and cut her in half, come out beyond her, piercing her like a butterfly, before she could have been his victim, and now he could be hers" (p. 138). The frontiers have become more intimate and dangerous as Harriet's desire, not just for sex but for revenge, brings to the surface feelings of racial hatred. When Arroyo knowingly, purposefully withholds his ejaculation during oral sex, she feels "damn him, damn the brown fucker, damn the ugly greaser, he refused because he wanted to strangle her, suffocate her . . . damn him, refusing to shrink and be beaten, refusing to acknowledge that in her mouth he was her captive" (pp. 138–139). This sex/murder fantasy in which she holds a part of him in her mouth, in her head, a part she fears is a weapon, ends with her "savage, guttural sound, the worst sound" (p. 139) she had ever emitted, and then his penis slaps against her; it "beat against her cheeks, flapping as she screamed, what is it with you, . . . you damned brown prick, what makes you refuse a woman a moment as free and powerful as the one you took before" (p. 139).

It is difficult to comment on this explosive sexual spectacle. Several questions might be more appropriate. What did Harriet expect when she finally let a man "have her at his pleasure"? And when she feels outrage in bed, is it realistic to think that it is only directed at General Arroyo? Could some of this outrage emerge from discovering the primal scene and then acting on it by being with both an "ugly greaser" (p. 138) and her father at the same time? From feeling the years of pent-up sexual desire finally accessible but somehow forbidden? Are her impulses for castration, focused here on the Mexican who withholds his orgasm and "equality" from her, completely confined to him? In this naked conflict of gender, race, and power, Fuentes etches the fate of this relationship — frustration and revenge.

INTERIOR SPECTACLES

"I think my father feels that in this moment he is a desperate apparition," states Christopher near the end of *Christopher Unborn* by Fuentes. *The Old Gringo* ends as it began, with the sentence "Now she sits alone and remembers" (p. 3). What Harriet has remembered is what Fuentes wants us to see as spectacles of border crossings between the conscious and unconscious minds, history and imagination, apparitions and memory. The power of the imagination resides not in its ability to always liberate history but to challenge the terror of history and gain an alternative reading of it. For who really crosses the frontiers of their differences with others and wins the battles with themselves in *The Old Gringo*? Those who, while having a memory, utilize it.

It is significant, when thinking about the interrelations of Fuentes' novels, that the last word of *Christopher Unborn* is "forgets." Whether remembering the revolution with Harriet Winslow or forgetting the world in gestation with Christopher, it is the imagination, the quality of the imagination with its apparitions, that counts, that gives us the opportunity to rethink the condition of our lives and the problems of human beings and their borders.

NOTES

1. The apparitions in Fuentes' novels are not limited to visions. He is drawn to all the senses and strives to include them in his work. In his essay "How I Started to Write" he states that Rimbaud's mother

    asked him what a particular poem was about. And [Rimbaud] answered: "I have wanted to say what it says there, literally and in all other senses." This statement of Rimbaud's has been an inflexible rule for me and for what we are all writing today; and the present-day vigor of literature in the Hispanic world, to which I belong, is not alien to this Rimbaudian approach to writing: Say what you mean, literally and in all other senses. (*Myself with Others: Selected Essays* [New York: Farrar, Straus & Giroux, 1988).

2. "Gabriel García Márquez and the Invention of America" in *Myself with Others*, p. 190.

3. I am using "apparition" in two senses: apparitions as appearances with a clear religious, otherworldly content and as images formed after the unconscious mind has reworked emotional experiences from childhood. Both kinds of apparitions, fortified by the senses of sight, hearing, and smell, can be experienced as exceptionally profound events tinctured with spiritual feeling.

4. By "transference" I mean "the displacement of patterns of feelings and behavior, originally experienced with significant figures of one's childhood, to individuals in one's current relationships. The unconscious process thus brings about a repetition, not consciously perceived, of attitudes, fantasies and emotions of love, hate, anger, etc. under many different circumstances." Burness E. Moore and Bernard D. Fine, eds., *A Glossary of Psychoanalytic Terms and Concepts* (New York: The American Psychoanalytic Association, 1968), p. 92.

5. By "primal scene" I mean something close to a "childhood recollection or a fantasy of a couple, usually father and mother, engaging in sexual intercourse. Whether the developing child has actually observed, or only imagined this scene, it is the focus of his subsequent curiosity regarding the physical nature of the intimate relationship between his parents" (ibid., p. 76). Such scenes often have a traumatic impact upon the subsequent emotional shape of a person's life. Later relationships can become emotionally tangled with the repressed memory of the primal scene.

6. More should be written on the subtle but pervasive power the anonymous Negress has in Harriet Winslow's life and in Fuentes' narration. A series of surrogate relationships are stimulated by the primal scene involving Harriet's white father and this black woman.

Women Writing in the Americas: New Projects of the 1980s

RAYMOND LESLIE WILLIAMS, *University of Colorado at Boulder*

The international recognition of the Latin American novel beginning in the 1960s was initially the heralding of male writers. Only recently have women writers, such as the Mexican Elena Poniatowska, the Argentine Luisa Valenzuela, and the Chilean Isabel Allende, become widely read beyond the following they already commanded in their respective countries. Nevertheless, women have played a historically prominent role in Latin American literary production. The rise of the feminist movement in the North Atlantic regions (or "industrialized West") during the 1960s and 1970s had considerable impact on Latin American women — to such an extent that by the early 1980s it became possible to speak of a self-consciously feminist Latin American novel. In addition, Ibero-Afro-Indo-American writers and critics have begun to theorize issues such as gender, power, and ideology in a variety of settings, including journals and books.[1] Four novelists who brought to bear a feminist project during the 1980s are the Colombian Albalucía Angel, the Chilean Diamela Eltit, the Argentine Susana Torres Molina, and the Brazilian Helena Parente Cunha.

This new feminist fiction of the 1980s is characterized by daring attitudes toward literary discourse and a direct questioning of dominant ideologies. Many of the women writers of the 1980s, Torres Molina, Angel, Eltit, and Parente Cunha included, are not only aware of their roles as women writers, but also are fully conscious of feminist theory. For the first time in Latin American fiction, the unmasking of ideology and the social construction of gender are carried out with a self-conscious and overt understanding of ideology and feminist theory. For example, the writers seek to understand the social and cultural practices that clarify how gender relations are constituted, reproduced, and contested. Each of the four writers under consideration seeks an understanding, in different

ways, of gender under patriarchal capitalism. Angel, Eltit, and Parente
Cunha share poststructuralist interests in the theory of language, subjectivity, and power as knowledge production.

Albalucía Angel is the author of five novels and one volume of
short fiction, not all of which should be identified with her new feminist
work. Her early writing reflects her experience living in Europe during
the 1960s. The novels *Los girasoles en invierno* (1970) and *Dos veces Alicia*
(1972) represent settings in the Europe with which she had just become
acquainted. In these works she only begins to explore how gender
relations are constituted. In *Estaba la pájara pinta sentada en el verde limón*
(1975), she returns to the experience of her youth in Colombia during
the period identified as La Violencia (approximately 1947 to 1958) and
becomes engaged in the analysis of power relations. Her experience in
Colombia and concern for power relations remain a central preoccupation in the short stories *¡Oh gloria inmarcesible!* (1979).

Angel's personal and professional interest in a self-conscious feminist writing during the 1980s is evident in the two novels *Misiá Señora*
(1982) and *Las andariegas* (1984). These are also her most hermetic
works. The protagonist of *Misiá Señora*, Mariana, is reared by a family
of the landed aristocracy in the coffee-growing region of Colombia. She
eventually finds herself caught between the expectations a patriarchal
capitalist society holds for young women — marriage, motherhood, and
reproduction — and a more marginal but potentially meaningful existence. Her friendships with Yosmina and Anaïs offer an alternative to
the patriarchal order.

The structure of *Misiá Señora*, divided into three parts, relates three
chronological stages of Mariana's life. These parts are formally identified
as *imágenes* (images). The first of these, entitled "Tengo una muñeca
vestida de azul" (I have a doll dressed in blue), deals with Mariana's
childhood and adolescence. The second, "Antigua sin sombra" (Ancient one without shadow), relates her courtship, marriage, her two
children's births, and her weakening mental state, which results in a stay
in a mental institution. The third *imágen*, "Los sueños del silencio"
(Dreams of silence), describes a series of dramatic visions that often
relate her to important female figures — her mother and grandmother.

Coming to an understanding of gender differences and female
identity is the central thematic thread of *Misiá Señora*. Much of the first
imágen deals with different aspects of female sexuality. Mariana's childhood contains the theme of the constitution of gender identity and

involves sexual harassment, initial experiences with machismo and, later, the gradual discovery of her own sexuality. The sexual harassment is a vague and incomprehensible experience for Mariana as a child and yet one of the significant images that she remembers in adulthood. The expression of machismo involves a variety of abusive experiences, including the portrayal of the traditional Latin American male role model as the assumed ideal.

In *Misiá Señora*, gender issues are also associated with the ideology of the Catholic church and with class structure. The protagonist's experience with the Catholic church involves her indoctrination as a child that the body represents sin — for example, the lesson that looking at someone nude was a sin ("mirar a alguien desnudo era pecado") and that touching her own body was also a sin. She lives with the legends of sexuality and sin as related to her by Catholic women. Later, as an adult herself, she struggles to overcome the intellectual barriers of this ideological indoctrination in order to contest the reproduction of the ideology. Her ideological awareness represents a first step in establishing a sense of her own sexual identity. When she loses her virginity, she thinks of all that the priests and monks had taught her as a child, and she feels the need to liberate herself from this past with the Church. Social class also affects the novel's presentation of gender issues: since Mariana belongs to the provincial aristocracy, she had been destined to become a passive and frivolous *niña linda* (pretty girl).

Misiá Señora is a novel whose feminism privileges the subjectivity of images and imagination, as defined by the work's tripartite structure. The protagonist, who occasionally assumes the role of writer, demonstrates a rampant imagination and proposes a search for a new feminine consciousness. As a child, Mariana's reaction to her identity crisis is to take refuge in her imagination. She pictures herself flying. As an adult, Mariana often interprets the concrete reality around her on the basis of her imagination. Consequently, in *Misiá Señora* the reader is presented a fictional world in which the line between reality and imagination is tenuous. One aspect of this highly imaginative experience is the creation of a new language — a feminine discourse — as part of Angel's feminist project.

Las andariegas is explicitly presented as a feminist work and is Angel's most radical experiment in fiction yet. It also represents a search. It is a search for an *écriture féminine* as well as an evocation of a woman's sense of courage. *Las andariegas* is also a postmodern project in the sense that it is a self-conscious attempt at fictionalizing poststructuralist feminist theory. It begins with two epigraphs, a statement by the author that sets forth the feminist project, and then a third epigraph. The first epigraph is from *Les guérrillères* by Monique Wittig and refers to women breaking the existing order and to their need for strength and courage. The second epigraph is from *Las nuevas cartas portuguesas* by Maria Isabel Barreno, Maria Teresa Horta, and Maria Velho da Costa and refers to women as firm and committed warriors. These two epigraphs are explained by the author's page-long statement, the third prefatory section to appear before the narrative. Angel relates that her reading of Wittig's *Les guérrillères* inspired her to undertake this project with women warriors who advance "desde ninguna región hacia la historia" (from nowhere to history). She uses images from stories of her childhood as a guide, transforming them into fables and cryptic visions. The final product of her search, according to Angel, is the hope that women have held throughout time. The third epigraph is from the mythology of a Colombian indigenous group, the Kogui, and emphasizes the role of the woman figure in creation.

Sixty-two brief anecdotes, rather than a plot line, fictionalize women who have been excised from history. They represent parables that heretofore have not been told in a woman's voice. The anecdotes relate the experiences of *viajeras* (traveling women) in an affirmative way.

The innovative language and experimental techniques of *Las andariegas* are an important aspect of its *écriture feminine*. Much of the narrative consists of brief phrases, often with unconventional punctuation. Rather than developing a consistent plot, these phrases often contain an image. The use of linguistic imagery is supported by visual images — a set of twelve drawings of women. Angel also experiments with the physical space of language in the text in a manner similar to the techniques of concrete poetry. The four pages of this type consist of a variety of circular and semicircular arrangements of the names of women famous in history. These four pages universalize the story of these constantly traveling women.

Las andariegas ends with a type of epilog consisting of another quotation from Monique Wittig, comprising four brief sentences that call for precisely the undertaking that is the essence of Angel's last two novels: a new language, a new beginning, and a new history for women. The author expresses optimism for this new beginning with the final sentence: "Ellas dicen que el sol va a salir" (They [feminine] say that the sun is going to come out). In summary, in her early work Angel is concerned mostly with issues of class; in the later work she develops a postmodern *écriture feminine*.

Diamela Eltit has published three novels and one short volume of documentary fiction. Her postmodern novelistic enterprise was born in the 1980s, after she began participating in cultural and political aspects of an underground resistance in Pinochet's Chile during the 1970s and early 1980s. The three novels, *Lumpérica* (1983), *Por la patria* (1986), and *El cuarto mundo* (1988), constitute a radical and experimental feminist project. Eltit believes that the effects of feminism are only beginning to be discernible in Latin American literature, for women writers have been at the periphery of literary histories controlled by men. She maintains that women's writing can bring a new criterion for the orders and disorders of language.

Lumpérica takes place in a public plaza in Santiago de Chile, has no real plot, and has as a main character "L. Iluminada." The characters' relationships to the physical space of the plaza and to language substitute for "action." In one rainy scene, the narrator states "No hay acciones posibles más que su propia lengua que aún, en lo propicio del ambiente, no surge" (There are no possible actions beyond language itself, in the setting itself, it doesn't come about). In addition to being a setting for a novel that never takes place, the plaza is the setting for a film, for there is the constant presence of a camera that films this self-conscious fiction/film. It is a self-conscious fiction/film because the characters and the situations are often discussed in the text as fictions and as part of a film. For example, the narrator states: "Este lumperío escribe y borra lo imaginario, se reparte las palabras, los fragmentos de letras, borran sus supuestos errores, ensayan sus caligrafías, endilgan el pulso, acceden a la imprenta" (This lumpen writes and erases the imaginary, distributes words, fragments of letters, erases the supposed errors, tries calligraphies, checks the pulse, cedes to print). More specifically, character and situations in *Lumpérica* frequently appear as social constructs under the constant analysis of the narrator or L. Iluminada. This self-conscious characterization as social constructs forms the connection between poststructuralist feminism and postmodernism. Each of the novel's ten chapters takes a radically different narrative strategy, with different types of language, organization, and even typography. The experimentation becomes progressively more intense as the novel develops, and chapters near the end of the novel are so experimental that their main subject, as in Angel's later work, becomes language itself. A minimal sense of coherence is created by the fact that the last chapter returns to the situation of the first, with L. Iluminada alone in the plaza, in contemplation.

The public plaza of Santiago de Chile in *Lumpérica* is a postmodern world of Jean Baudrillard, where human beings have the same exchange value as merchandise, "as commercial products" and "as merchandise of uncertain value." As the scenes in the novel are filmed and discussed, these conversations recall Baudrillard's admonition that "there is no longer any medium in the literal sense: it is now intangible, diffuse and diffracted in the real, and it can no longer even be said that the latter is distorted by it" (p. 54). The novel is populated by the urban lumpen of the public plaza, who are identified as *desarropados* (poorly clothed). These marginalized groups — including figures such as prostitutes, homosexuals, transvestites, beggars, and alcoholics — have been the main thematic focus of the Chilean painters and photographers of Eltit's generation known as *la avanzada*. This interest confirms Linda Hutcheon's statement that "The different and the paradoxical fascinate the postmodern" (p. 47).

Lumpérica is a novel of *precarias verdades* — unstable, unsure, provisional truths. Even the anecdotes that are told in the novel are contingent and provisional. Truth becomes the object of manipulation in the seventh chapter, which consists of an unidentified *interrogador* questioning an unidentified *interrogado* about a seemingly insignificant event that takes place on the public plaza, when L. Iluminada apparently falls and the *interrogado* comes to her aid briefly. The *interrogador* repeatedly questions the *interrogado* about this until the latter finally changes his story, in a replica of an interview of political prisoners under dictatorships such as Pinochet's.

Eltit's second work, *Por la patria*, is her most ambitious novel to date and has been appropriately called a "reading of the history of our language and of the successive layers of its memory" (Brito, p. 209). In effect, Eltit relates a story of contemporary Chile revolving around the political repression of the Pinochet regime but always examining the historical origins of language, repression, and resistance. Returning to the medieval epic wars, she associates these historical conflicts to the contemporary situation. Consequently, Eltit's postmodern is patently historical and political. By exploring the origins of the "mother language" and incorporating numerous historical and colloquial languages into *Por la patria*, Eltit considers the insidious relationship between language and power.

Eltit is interested in the concept of "linguistic incest." As a point of departure, this problem relates to the fact that postmodern fiction poses new questions about reference. As Hutcheon points out, the question is no longer "to what empirically real object in the past does the language of history refer?"; it is more "to which discursive context could this language belong? To which prior textualizations must we refer?" (Hutcheon, p. 119). *Lumpérica* and *Por la patria* reveal a sense for origins in the Latin language, the mother language of the later Romance language family, a family present in both novels. The discursive contexts change in the different fragments of *Lumpérica*; again, referring to Latin and with resonances of medieval Spanish and Italian. These different historical languages coexist, in an unresolved contradiction, with a more current masculine discourse subverted by other contemporary discourses — colloquial Chilean Spanish and feminine discourse. The juxtaposition of these languages could be seen as the "linguistic incest" in the linguistic family that inhabits this novel.

Eltit's third novel, *El cuarto mundo* (1988), centers on a family and is related by two narrators: the first half of the work by a young boy, María Chipia, the son of the family, and the second half by his twin sister. Both sections deal with the relationships among the five members of the family: the twins, a younger sister (María de Alava), and the two parents. The first part of the novel ends with a family crisis centered on the mother's adultery. In the second part, the family tensions center on the incestuous relationship between María Chipia and his twin sister. She becomes pregnant and continues her relationship with him as the crisis continues to grow near the end of the novel. Only in the last line is the pregnant twin sister identified by name: diamela eltit [*sic*].

El cuarto mundo is not a work of the broad historical truths elaborated in Gabriel García Márquez' *One Hundred Years of Solitude* or Carlos Fuentes' *The Death of Artemio Cruz*. The generation of Fuentes and García Márquez remained not only overtly historical, but engaged in conveying the truths of social emancipation. *El cuarto mundo*, however, is about other kinds of truths — the truths of private and public space, the truths of relationships, the truths of the body, and a questioning of the possibilities language holds for articulating truths. They are the relative truths of Baudrillard's postmodern and, in this sense, Eltit questions the assumptions of the totalizing modernist undertaking of the previous generation of Latin American writers.

María Chipia begins narrating the novel as a fetus, and much of his narration consists of his attempt to understand the relationship of his own body to his mother's and his sister's. Consequently, it is a story of subtle spaces and of constantly changing personal distances. As a child in the cradle, he states that the *miradas* (looks) fixed on him lead him to dislike public spaces. As a one-year-old, María Chipia sees a world of chaos around him and thinks that language will provide order. Nevertheless, he soon realizes that language will be the least viable vehicle for communicating orders and truths. By age three, for example, María Chipia understands that the idea of any transcendent meaning of language was a fantasy. Rather, his truths are found and then discarded within the different spaces in which he operates. For example, as a young adolescent he lives the desire for the space of a masculine paradise outside the home dominated by his mother, but he eventually realizes that such a space is yet another truth impossible for him to attain. Once he begins the incestuous relationship with his sister, he faces the novel's most complex truth: that he is a *sudaca*, a derogatory term for Latin Americans used by Spaniards. María Chipia constantly repeats that he is a *sudaca*, a dignified *sudaca*. In the end, the most notable truths in *El cuarto mundo* are *verdades sudacas*, "sudaca truths," degraded truths. The narrator "diamela eltit" observes her mother and her sister near the end of the novel and describes a postmodern condition of a "*degradada humanidad sudaca*" (degraded *sudaca* humanity). As she nears birth and crisis at the end of the novel, she also describes her mother and sister as "*perros sudacas*" (*sudaca* dogs).

On the final page of *El cuarto mundo*, it is evident that the entire situation consists of degradation, commercialization, reification. The novel's last sentence states: "La niña sudaca irá a la venta" (The *sudaca* girl will go up for sale). The newly born child going up for sale belongs to the postmodern society of Fredric Jameson's late capitalism and Baudrillard's postmodernism, one in which abstract qualities like goodness and knowledge enter into the realm of exchange value. And we can include "truth" in these abstract values, which becomes degraded and meaningless in this *sudaca* world, as does language.

Dueña y señora by Susana Torres Molina is not as formally innovative as Angel's and Eltit's novels, but this volume of short stories represented a major breakthrough in contemporary Argentine writing when it began to circulate in Buenos Aires in 1983. Never before had an Argentine woman writer published such sexually explicit and audacious fiction. The lesbian sexual encounters in *Dueña y señora* scandalized Argentina's conservative reading public as much as Enrique Medina's irreverent and sexually daring novels had a decade earlier. Never before had a woman Argentine celebrated the female body and lesbianism in such a fashion. Its shock value aside, Torres Molina's central focus is how gender relations are constituted, reproduced, and contested.

Dueña y señora consists of a prolog written by Martha Berlin, followed by nine stories told in the first person by Torres Molina. Several of the early stories question and subvert the traditional gender relations established by Argentina's patriarchal order. Many of the stories portray a woman's celebration of sexuality and pleasure. This feminist perspective is similar to the position of the cultural feminists in the United States.[2] The last story, "Impresiones de una futura mamá," is a celebration of lesbianism. In her prolog, Berlin sets forth one of the key points and constant concerns of this volume, pointing out that women have not had the opportunity to "name the spaces of pleasure" (nominar los espacios del goce). Berlin also questions the ideological implications of the Argentine colloquial phrases *verdaderas mujeres* (true women) and *verdaderos hombres* (true men). In addition, she describes Torres Molina as a writer who is fully conscious of her ideological agenda.

These nine stories are not particularly "well written," either in the traditional sense of "well-crafted fiction" (*buen escribir*) or in the modern sense of being technically innovative. The language appears simple and colloquial; the style is clearly the most "antiliterary" of the four writers. Nevertheless, these fictions subtly undermine the traditional sense of gender relations, including much of the everyday and colloquial language intimately associated with traditional sex roles. In the first story, "El bicho canasto," Torres Molina subverts the patriarchal Latin American tradition of the *piropo* — the verbal harassment of women in public places. The female protagonist is harassed on the street by a male who articulates progressively more vulgar *piropos*, but in the end, she reverses the traditional sex roles and intimidates him in a surprising turn of events: she returns even more aggressive and vulgar *piropos* to him.

The publication of Torres Molina's *Dueña y señora* marked an important turning point for women's writing in Argentina and in Latin America in general: for the first time a woman had published a book with an explicitly lesbian content.³ Torres Molina's writing functions along the lines of what some feminists in the United States have called cultural feminism. Promoted by feminists such as Mary Daly and Adrienne Rich, it is the ideology of a female nature or female essence reappropriated by women themselves in an effort to revalidate undervalued female attributes. In "Impresiones de una futura mamá," Torres Molina aligns herself with the cultural feminists, for she celebrates female biological differences. Unlike other feminists, such as Angel, for the cultural feminists the enemy of women is not merely a social system, an economic institution, or a set of backward beliefs, but masculinity itself and in some cases male biology. Torres Molina also questions the social system and its reproduction of patriarchal social codes. Like Angel, she is engaged in the analysis of gender-based power relations, for they are the primary focus of most of these stories.

Helena Parente Cunha, a professor of literary theory at the Universidade Federal in Rio de Janeiro, published her first novel, *Mulher no espelho*, written in Portuguese in 1983. (The English translation, *Woman Between Mirrors*, was brought out in 1989.) Given her background in literary theory, Parente Cunha is more similar to Angel and Eltit in some ways than to Torres Molina. Previously unknown as a writer in Brazil, Parente Cunha in this work demonstrated interest in psychoanalytic models of sexuality and subjectivity. *Woman Between Mirrors* is an experiment in privileging the subjective in constituting the meaning of a middle-aged woman's lived reality. The protagonist is a forty-five-year-old Brazilian married to an extraordinarily dominant Brazilian man. She also has three teenage sons. The narrative is her response to the otherness of female sexuality that has been repressed by the patriarchy.

The woman begins by relating anecdotes from her youth. She tells her life story in a basically linear fashion, although she does alternate between the past and the present. In her earliest childhood memories, she recalls competition with her brother, who received more attention than she from her parents. As a child she always respected the patriarchal order, assuming a role inferior to her brother and being totally subservient to her father. She has played a similar role with her husband, an alcoholic woman chaser who eventually becomes a physically repugnant and boring figure for her. In addition to her multiple fantasies about the ideal lover, she actually has an affair — with the man whose wife is having an affair with her husband. By the end of the novel, the protagonist is successfully reworking the terms of her existence.

Woman Between Mirrors is an innovative work, and its most interesting technical device is the constant presence of a voice identified as "the woman who writes me." This voice appears in italicized type in passages ranging from a sentence to several lengthy paragraphs. "The woman who writes me" is an oppositional voice that frequently questions the protagonist's thoughts, actions, and motives. In the early stages, this voice plays the role of an analytical psychologist, questioning the protagonist's true motives, even though the latter claims that she has invented and controls this fictional voice. The protagonist also states that the woman who writes her never gets out of her control. Nevertheless, the relationship between the two involves a constant power struggle.

In this novel, the act of writing functions as a paradigm of power relationships. The protagonist struggles with "the woman who writes me" just as she struggles with her husband. She gradually takes control of her entire situation, exercising power over both the woman who writes her and her husband. She also establishes identity by rediscovering the African culture of Brazil that had been forbidden when she was a child. (The image of the mango tree appears throughout the novel in association with this repressive childhood.) At the end of the novel she describes herself as whole and multiple.

Woman Between Mirrors is a heterogeneous and theoretically self-conscious work that is typical of some of the most engaging feminist novels written in Latin America during the 1980s. Parente Cunha has put into practice Hélène Cixous' admonition to "write yourself. Your body must be heard." Consequently, this Brazilian writer, like Torres Molina, also aligns herself with the cultural feminists in the United States who believe in an essence of female biology.

*   *   *

These four writers, their feminist projects all arising during the early 1980s, represent a radical change in the type of feminist writing to be found in Latin America. Each of the four writers proposes an *écriture feminine*. Angel and Eltit undertake the most radical attempt at attaining this feminine discourse in *Las andariegas* and *Por la patria*, respectively, with their search for an innovative language and imagery. In contrast, Torres Molina's *écriture feminine* consists of a patently antiliterary language. Parente Cunha finds her own *écriture feminine* through the presence of "the woman who writes me."

The four writers engage in the unmasking of ideology and the social construction of reality. They subvert the construction of power relationships with a variety of strategies. In *Las andariegas* and *Por la patria*, Angel and Eltit propose newly gendered structures of power. Torres Molina creates women characters who directly question the power relationships implied in Latin American machismo. Parente Cunha's subversive counterdiscourse is articulated through "the woman who writes me," who becomes empowered by the end of the novel.

With the rise of these four writers, it is evident that the generation of Latin American novelists after the "boom" offers a variety of aesthetic and political agendas different from the 1960s. Angel, Eltit, Torres Molina, and Parente Cunha represent a new feminist agenda in Latin American fiction of the 1980s and 1990s.

NOTES

1. Examples of the new journals and magazines dealing with feminist issues are *El debate feminista* and *Fem* in Mexico, *Feminaria* in Argentina, and *Revista de crítica cultural* in Chile. Just a few examples of recent feminist literary studies to appear in Latin America are those by Araújo, Bradu, García Pinto, González and Ortega, and Silva-Velázquez and Erro-Orthman. In addition, Foster (1991) has recently published *Gay and Lesbian Themes in Latin American Writing*.

2. Alcoff has discussed cultural feminism in great detail .

3. Foster (1989) has discussed the importance of Torres Molina's fiction in the Argentine and Latin American context.

WORKS CITED

Alcoff, Linda. 1988. "Cultural Feminism versus Poststructuralism: The Identity Crisis in Feminist Theory." *Signs: Journal of Women in Culture and Society* 13, no. 3: 405–436.

Angel, Albalucía. 1970. *Los girasoles en invierno*. Bogotá: Bolívar.

———. 1972. *Dos veces Alicia*. Barcelona: Seix-Barral.

———. 1975. *Estaba la pájara pinta sentada en el verde limón*. Bogotá: Instituto Colombiano de Cultura.

———. 1982. *Misiá Señora*. Barcelona: Argos Vergara.

———. 1984. *Las andariegas*. Barcelona: Argos Vergara.

Araújo, Helena. 1989. *La scherezada criolla: Ensayos sobre escritura feminina latinoameri-cana*. Bogotá: Universidad Nacional de Colombia.

Baudrillard, Jean. 1983. *Simulations*. New York: Semiotext(e).

Bradu, Fabienne. 1987. *Señas particulares: Escritora*. México: Fondo de Cultura.

Brito, Eugenia. 1990. *Campos Minados: literatura post-globe en Chile*. Santiago: Editorial Cuarto Propio.

Eltit, Diamela. 1983. *Lumpérica*. Santiago de Chile: Ediciones del Ornitorrinco.

———. 1986. *Por la patria*. Santiago de Chile: Edicones del Ornitorrinco.

———. 1988. *El cuarto mundo*. Santiago de Chile: Planeta.

Foster, David William. 1989. "The Manipulation of the Horizons of Reader Expectation in Two Examples of Argentine Lesbian Writing: Discourse Power and Alternate Sexuality." University of Colorado, Spanish and Portuguese Distinguished Lecture Series 8-9 (Spring): 117–127.

———. 1991. *Gay and Lesbian Themes in Latin American Writing*. Austin: University of Texas Press.

García Pinto, Magdalena. 1988. *Historias íntimas: Conversaciones con diez escritoras latinoamericanas*. Hanover, N.H.: Ediciones del Norte.

González , Patricia Elena, and Eliana Ortega, editors. 1984. *La sarten por el mango*. San Juan: Ediciones del Huracán.

Hutcheon, Linda. 1988. *A Poetics of Postmodernism: History, Theory, Fiction*. London: Routledge.

Parente Cunha, Helena. 1989. *Woman Between Mirrors*. Trans. Fred P. Ellison and Naomi Lindstrom. Austin: University of Texas Press.

Silva-Velázquez , Caridad L., and Nora Erro-Orthman. 1986. *Puerta abierta: La nueva escritora latinoamericana*. Mexico City: Joaquín Mortiz.

Torres Molina, Susana. 1983. *Dueña y señora*. Buenos Aires: Ediciones La Campana.

Unwriting

RONALD SUKENICK, *University of Colorado at Boulder*

I suddenly realized this morning, without needing to think about it much because once you realize it it becomes trivial and sort of obvious, why I like the creative methods of the early twentieth-century French eccentric Raymond Roussel, but reject, at least for myself, the similar methods of his followers in the contemporary Oulipo group. It's because Roussel used arbitrary methods of composition to free himself from the conventional, while Oulipo uses the same techniques as conventions in themselves, however idiosyncratic. Oulipo is formalist; Roussel was supremely antiformalist.

I'm an admirer of many of the Oulipo writers — Queneau and Calvino, of course, but also Perec and Harry Matthews, for example. It's just that I'm a different kind of writer, one who has never been much concerned with form, unless to break down other forms, thereby creating a vacuum inviting new material. Oulipo methods do the same thing, it's true, but then, a convention established, repeat programmatically, where an antiformalist like myself would go on to improvise as in a jazz solo, picking up on the last phrase and going from there. It's just a difference, the difference, say, between Bach and Bird.

Rather than subscribe, like a good modernist, merely to Gide's advice to "follow the word," I have also considered the word as that which follows. Which is partly just to say, I guess, that I'm American rather than French, or even European. Gary Cooper more than John Gielgud. Marlon Brando more than Barrault. Pollock more than Braque. Language is what follows from experience and is just another kind of experience. One to be wary of, considering its power. To distrust. Not the matrix or template of experience, or if it is you're in trouble. Certainly not language as holy writ, the way it is in Paris.

And form, too, like language, is after the fact. Form is just an extension of content, as in the Creeley-Olson formulation.

This, for me, is simply the difference between Europe and the United States, and possibly also a difference between the States and Latin America, insofar as it's influenced by Europe. Because in the States the rules don't apply. You have to improvise your own rules. Or so we seem to deeply believe. Even though clearly not always true, sometimes the rules are there and we persist in ignoring them; this is our characteristic failing. But often true. Crucially so.

But also, maybe it's the difference between the Greco-Christian tradition and the Jewish tradition — and possibly other non-Western traditions as well. Language does not imitate experience, as in the classical tradition. It does not constitute the limits of experience, as in France. No. Language is one kind of experience, but a kind so powerful that it has an unusual capacity to form and deform other kinds of experience.

Powerful because if language is after the fact, it is simultaneously before the fact. Maybe, in fact, it is the fact, as some contend. Or if it isn't, it's hard to tell the difference, because what is the status of fact before it's coded into language? Shaky. Ephemeral at best, beyond consciousness at worst. Nevertheless, it's a writer's job, in my opinion, to try. To unwrite the book of life till the difference between language and the rest of experience is as clear as possible before we write fact into language again.

Which brings me to the idea of unwriting. I guess I'd have to argue that unwriting is more critical than writing — meaning "critical" here in both its senses. Any literate fool can write; only writers know how to unwrite what is written. Not, obviously, that writing is any less important. Language has to be written before it can be unwritten. Writing is the crucial step culture takes out of the ephemera of experience into historical existence. The disproportionate influence of Jews, who are key figures in recent French and Franco-American language philosophy, privileging writing over speech, is maybe not coincidental.

The advantages of history, looking at it with an innocent eye, are enormous, the chief among them being that you can think about it in some continuous and organized way. And thinking about it you can revise it. And revising it you can participate in creating a future, which is basically no other than more history. Just as "creative" writing can generate experience — experience that did not exist before the creative act. Experience "real" enough to intervene in the book of life, to modify experience as it evolves. Which explains the potential prophetic power of this kind of writing.

And by the way, the metaphor of a book of life is itself a deeply Jewish idea. Life itself is a kind of writing. And God has both the pencil and the eraser. "He who has sinned against Me, him only will I erase from My record."

You can see that I am evolving a recipe here for endurance and growth, for a mode of dealing with experience that can thrive even on its own disasters. It's the kind of thing that sustains we Jews and incites anti-Semites to tantrums and paranoia. Nevertheless, it looks like we're heading toward a notion that might be called talmudic fiction.

What said creative act deals in is what I've called unwriting. Every such act unwrites what has been formulated as experience to allow a new sense of experience to evolve. Which once assimilated will itself need to be unwritten. You need both the pencil and the eraser. This is not an activity limited by any means to the so-called creative arts. A more inclusive term for it would be "commentary."

Nor is it limited to language. Nor is writing limited to language. Any practice of graphics, any fabrication of imagery can be a kind of writing, so long as it is not representational. Thus Jackson Pollock is a kind of writer. Plato was right — representation is taboo. Through mimetic representation writing becomes imitative, secondhand, fake, a desecration of experience. And, de facto, self-contradictory in the face of what it represents.

But Plato is also wrong for our age, or rather, dealt with a, for us, incomplete spectrum. We have to consider the obvious possibility of imagery without imitation. After a century of abstract art, after the triumph of the digital computer, which proceeds by abstraction — over the analog computer, which proceeds by modeling, miming, its information — this is an option that it's ignorant to ignore. The Second Commandment gets it right: no graven images, OF anything. Of ANY-THING. And that includes electronic images.

Otherwise you end up with a fetish, the Golden Calf. Which is what we usually end up with the way things are currently set up.

The image that is not fetishized, however, is a different story. The unfetishized image is not imitation of reality but simply more reality. The unfetishized image is not something that can be mass produced. It is improvised and unrepeatable. It is articulated in the stream of time and, impossible to reify, thingify, disappears downstream. It cannot become a commodity. It is the precise opposite of Andy Warhol's terminal parody of the fetishized image in our culture of mass-produced multiples. Is it completely coincidental that Henry Ford was a vicious anti-Semite?

Traditionally in Jewish culture one does not speak the name of God. To name is to fetishize. To fetishize is to limit. To limit is to paralyze. The power of the graven image, the idol, the Golden Calf, is the monolithic power of stasis. Oppression. The power of the nameless principle is the power of accommodation and change, which is also the innate power of language. Language is implicitly iconoclastic. Even if you try to ignore or stifle that power, it will come back at you. The master who saw that American discourse had unleashed this power, in common with some non-Western cultures, was Emerson. In 1844 his essay "The Post" appeared. Emerson in this essay represents the initial and, if you take him seriously, final break of the North American literary tradition from that of Europe.

To a writer in this tradition, as Emerson says, all ideas are wrong, because ideas are frozen thought. This puts ideologues in an uncomfortable position, and maybe goes some way to explain the incomprehension gap between U.S. artists and intellectuals. Intellectuals are concerned with Thought; Emerson was concerned with thinking. It follows that all fixed forms are negations. Negation of possibility. Negation, even, of the spirit, what I might call mind, by the illusory urge to fix it, quantify it, thingify it. The motto of American intellectuals is: if it works, fix it. Whereas, as Wallace Stevens says somewhere, the poet is the man whose mind is never made up.

This is not an essay against form, mind you. It's an essay against fixed form, maybe. Preconceived form. Not against fabrication but prefabrication. An essay for a notion that Robbe-Grillet once advanced, that the form of a given work, or at least novel, should be unique and unrepeatable. That — by extension — no successful work can be formally defined before the fact of its creation, nor can its form define any subsequent work.

Provisional. Contingent. Problematic. Contentious. These are the terms that I associate with American writing at its characteristic best, and that includes AmericaN fictions as well as fiction of the AmericaS. These are also the terms I associate with talmudic commentary. These, I think I can say now, looking back, are the qualities I have always been groping for, with much backtracking and digression, in the contemporary shitstorm of ideas about what fiction is supposed to be. They roughly indicate my habit of thought, my native style, from which almost my entire formal education, out of a different habit of thought, Greco-Christian, has tended to wear me. And these are qualities that are slowly coming to be valued, and to a certain degree have always been recognized in our writers, but with an appreciation that resembles a rubber band — the sensibility stretches for a Faulkner or a Barthelme almost despite itself, then snaps back into old habits. But the rubber band is getting old, losing its elasticity, and one day in stretching will simply break. At that point so-called mainstream fiction, thought to be a preeminent style, will be recognized as simply a function of the corporate market. As such, there is no reason it shouldn't continue to be produced and sold. "Product," as they call it in the industry.

The way things are now, however, you can buy a hundred different kinds of breakfast cereal in the shopping malls of America, but only one kind of novel. That's a consequence of the corporate market, which is not a free market. In a corporate market, corporations are free to impose. In a free market, consumers are free to choose.

Think about the uses of written language other than representation and you get some sense of the narrow exclusivity of what is called mainstream fiction in the States. Giving directions, writing prescriptions, laying curses, recording transactions, blowing off steam, invoking mysteries, registering wishes, spinning fantasies, venting rage, expressing grief, rationalizing behavior, flaunting compulsions, inciting activity, interpreting laws, performing magic, promoting seductions, creating legends, coining phrases, arguing politics, playing games, defending justice, drafting epistles, spreading lore, evoking joy, analyzing ideas, urging morality, arousing desire, predicting the future, exposing vice, encouraging visions, bullshitting, revenge, boasting, remembering, boosting, beatifying, billing and cooing, believing, burning up, blissing out, and I'm only up to the b's.

It strikes me as I write that the variety of this list resembles the variety of talmudic commentary. None of these require plot, character, and description. No mimesis. That's just Greek to me. Story, maybe, but narrative is so endemic to thought itself that when you ask about narrative you have to start from the other end of the question: what is there that is not narrative? Most people think in narrative, and departures from it in the form of reasoned or logical discourse take off from that ongoing story we tell ourselves, more or less like arias or soliloquies.

And, conversely, from this point of view, it turns out that narrative is a kind of thinking.

The coming changes in AmericaN fiction — and here I am intentionally hemispheric — are not in the province of an avant-garde, which is obviously a European conception that doesn't apply to the case. These are changes that have a demographic and popular base. They will reflect the basic changes in society under way because of population shifts, ethnic alterations, technological advances, economic upheavals. Some of them will not be to my liking, but that's sort of beside the point. They comprise an unruly horse we will have to ride, and the only way to handle it will be to try to understand it.

Democracy is unruly and likes to conceive itself as unruly, but it is not unpersuadable when it comes to rules. We admire the outlaw, the Lone Ranger, but it turns out that the outlaw abides by a superior law for which we yearn. And that superior law, is it not, is what our creative discourse, our communal commentary ideally argues toward. As the Talmud argues Mosaic law, so we contend toward a law that, given our diversity, will need to be a law of mosaics. That is the implicit end of the story, which admittedly will never end. Removing that implicit goal would make outlaws of us all.

So maybe the manifestation of our collective story that we are used to calling fiction, however you want to define it, is a reflection of that communal narrative, and at best is one of the forces that helps to shape it.

Which brings us to the post-European novel. Even Europeans are starting to write it. The post-European novel is less a phenomenon of place than of time. The traditional Euro-American novel was an esthetic entity confined to that cultural zoo called The Arts, section of Imagination, in the cage labeled Literary. Alongside the fabrications of Disneyland. However, the time does not require an imagination that fabricates but a narrative that deals with hard data, that weaves together the disturbingly present strands of a shredded cultural fabric into a coat of many colors. In western Europe some of the most interesting cultural developments seem to concern the effort of former colonial peoples to emerge into the mainstream of formerly colonialist countries. In the United States and Canada populations that once would have disappeared into the melting pot now insist on cohabitation within a mosaic. The force of mestizo culture in Latin America has always been strong and will inevitably get stronger.

It is getting hard to make an argument for an oppositional "outsider" culture now because the inside is beginning to disappear; harder to speak of a legitimate avant-garde at the cutting edge because the edge is moving toward the center rather than out into unexplored territory. There are few virgin forests, and those that remain need to be protected rather than explored. No more noble savages, no more escape from civilization. We are all cultivators now, and we have little choice but to cultivate. And be cultivated. Civilization or, possibly, nothing. We live in a society of lawyers rather than outlaws. The job of the writer in such a milieu would appear to be litigious and even liturgical. "Rabbi, rabbi, fend my soul for me,/ And the true savant of this dark nature be."

And in doing so, get us out of this cage called Literature.

Manifesto in Voices

RIKKI DUCORNET, *University of Denver*

L'homme est descendu du signe.
— Matta

France's Uqbar, the Mas d'Azil in the Pyrénées, was once truffled with painted stones. It is supposed that these represent lunar notations. Deeper in the mountains, in the Valley of Marvels, a seemingly infinite number of drawings and engravings — maps, beasts, beings, and moons — animate the rock. These are the embryos of language: telesma, perfect things, and the potencies which once served to ignite the imaginations of our most distant ancestors. Europe and Africa, Asia, Australia and Middle America — all our fictions are seeded here, in mountains and in valleys, in such figures painted on stone — visions of the hunt, vivid reveries, barbed wands, red footprints that show the direction a narrative must take, the demons of storms, vulvas self-contained and swollen like bells.

"The word is our sign and seal," writes Octavio Paz. "By means of it we recognize each other among strangers" (*The Labyrinth of Solitude*).

What follows is about recognition, the sacred nature of the word, that "magical ambiguity" (Paz) which gives wings to the beast and meanings to the moon.

"Let us imagine something yellow," Borges invites us, "shining, changing. That thing is something in the sky, circular; at other times it has the form of an arc, other times it grows and shrinks. Someone — our common ancestor — gives to that thing the name of moon, different in different languages, and variously lovely" (*Seven Nights*).

"Now it is night," (and the voice is George Lamming's, the book: *The Castle of My Skin*); "now it is night with the moon sprinkling its light on everything. The wood is a thick shroud of leaves asleep, and the sleep, like a fog, conceals those who within the wood must keep awake."

*   *   *

Let us imagine that the novel is a species of variable moon and wakeful — its wilderness mapped by Alejo Carpentier, its borderlands plotted by Clarice Lispector, its body dreamed by Severo Sarduy, its atlases bound by Asturias, its circumference squared by Ray Federman, its pantries stocked by Harry Mathews, its songs sung by The Mighty Sparrow, its tigers Borgesian and which — if they can be taught to dance — refuse to carry the cumbersome baggage of orthodoxy. Let us imagine the novel as a kind of "savage beast (that springs upon us) not to rend but to rescue us from death" (W. H. Hudson, *Green Mansions*).

Not long ago the Canadian novelist Barry Callaghan was threatened by a woman (white) who expressed the intention to decock him for having written in a voice other than his own — that of a woman (black). Shortly thereafter, I, too, was aggressed for a similar offense — a character in one of my novels is an Amazonian Indian, something I am not. Next, and within the hour, I witnessed a young writer asking permission of other writers to finish her book:

"I am female, heterosexual and white," she said, "yet my novel is narrated by a male homosexual who is Chinese. Do I have the right to continue?"

In answer, I propose these words of Wilson Harris: "I view the novel as a kind of infinite canvas. By infinity I mean that one is constantly breaking down things in order to sense a vision through things. And that applies to characters as well" (*Kas Kas*).

Like the moon, the novel is a symbol and a necessary reality. Ideally it serves neither gods nor masters. Philosopher's stone, it sublimates, precipitates, and quickens. House of Keys, it opens all our darkest doors. May the Pol Pot Persons of all genders and denominations take heed: to create a fictional world with rigor and passion, to imagine a character of any sex, place, time, or color and make it palpitate and quiver, to catapult it into the deepest forests of our most luminous reveries, is to commit an act of empathy. To write a novel of the imagination is a gesture of tenderness; to enter into the body of a book is a fearless act and generous.

"What is forged in the secret act of reading," says Salman Rushdie, is "a different kind of identity, as the reader and writer merge. . . . This 'secret identity' . . . is the novel form's greatest and most subversive gift . . . [and] why I elevate the novel above all other forms, why it has always been, and remains my first love: not only is it the art involving the least compromises, but it is also the only one that takes 'the privileged arena' of conflicting discourses right inside our heads. The interior space of our imagination is a theatre that can never be closed down" (*Brick*).

Although it can:

"In the Gestapo cellars," George Steiner reminds us (in *Language and Silence*), "stenographers (usually women) took down the noises of fear and agony wrenched, burned, or beaten out of the human voice." In those cellars, the little stones of potencies, lunar alphabets, rampant bestiaries, and the sacred seeds of recognition — were reduced to dirt.

Steiner proposes (as does Alice Miller — one of the lights behind Russell Banks' extraordinary new novel *Affliction*) that our century, its great wars, pogroms, and holocausts, are the fulfillment of the previous century's most malignant wishes, an aspiration for perversity and a passion for chaos. It is no accident that the great novels of the 1980s are informed by tragedy, the recognition of finitude, of Total Eclipse. (Again, *Affliction* comes to mind, and *Midnight's Children*, and *Beloved*; *The Kiss Of The Spider Woman* and *Gerald's Party*. . . .)

"Calamity," says Robert Coover, "is the normal circumstance of the universe." "We have come to the end of a tradition," Coover continues. "I don't mean to say that we have come to the end of the novel . . . but that our ways of looking at the world . . . are changing" (*The Metafictional Muse*).

Mystics and physicists alike tell us that moons and tigers — all matter, inert and quickened — are made of the same reeling particles. We move through the maze of the world, and the world's maze moves through us. An intergalactic observer might judge us far less attractive than our cousins the other apes (and it is the baboons, after all, who are blessed with iridescent faces and behinds) — but ours is the species capable of acting with responsibility and an informed heart. Yet, with every volatilized jungle tree (and a species that burns its own cannot be expected to respect the lives of plants, to take the time to decode the conversations, perhaps philosophical, of elephants, creatures apparently aware, as are we, of finitude) — we prefer to pursue folly, and with an autophageous appetite.

"What we ask of writers," says Italo Calvino, "is that they guarantee survival of what we call human in a world where everything appears inhuman." And he continues: "Literature is like an ear that can hear beyond the understanding of the language of politics" (*The Uses Of Literature*).

I insist: it is not only our right, but our responsibility to follow our imaginations' enchanted paths wherever they would lead us; to heed those voices which inhabit our most secret (and sacred) spaces. When in 1973 thousands were taken to Santiago Stadium to be tortured to death (and artists and writers were among the first to be arrested by Pinochet's illegal government), Gabriel García Márquez, in an act of defiance and revulsion, ceased to write. After five years, he "came to the conclusion that only by writing could I oppose Pinochet. Without realizing it, I had submitted myself to his censorship" (*Nouvelle Observateur*).

"Literature" (and the voice is that of Luisa Valenzuela), "is the site of the cross-waters — the murky and clear waters where nothing is exactly in its place because there is no precise place. We have to invent it each time" (*Little Manifesto*).

It is precisely this capacity for invention which makes the world worth wanting. The capacity to dream very high dreams and to sing — as did the ancients of Dreamtime — songs potent enough to engender a universe. Those who ask us to deny our dreams would pillage our valley of marvels, would reduce our lunar notations to ashes, would flay our vivid tigers, would deny that the frontiers of the novel, our first love, are infinite.

"When we are aware of our disease or hidden motives" (Italo Calvino), "we have already begun to get the better of them. What matters is the way in which we accept our motives and live through the ensuing crises. This is the only chance we have of becoming different from the way we are — that is the only way of starting to invent a new way of being."

On Literary Creation

DIAMELA ELTIT, *Santiago de Chile*

THE IMPOSSIBLE

From my point of view, working in the field of symbolic creation — such as literature — implies a certain impossibility of providing a precise accounting of the laws that govern writing, laws that dictate a given narrative decision, a thematic field, or the markings of an aesthetic destiny, for example. And it is impossible to account for these laws because the symbolic organization that literary writing entails is so extensive and therefore incomprehensible, while so multiple that any attempt to define it is merely a reductive gesture, a simplified parody of the energy that makes it possible, an asphyxiated reference to its land-scape, barely a semblance of its passage.

Nevertheless, what does seem possible to me is to examine the objectivity of one part of literary creation: that which, while it tells a particular story, also reveals a political choice through the writing of that language. If we accept that language is not innocent, rather that it is loaded by the moving game of history (in the sense of "History" and biographical history, intertwined in social change); if we agree to the possibility of thinking that literature (and writing) exhibits the symp-toms of immoderation — by its diverse economy, by its metaphoric range — and that its meaning demands to reveal precisely the meanings of language, through the social possibilities of the text, then one may examine, in my estimation, the political filiation of a work.

WHAT IS ANOTHER'S, WHAT IS DISTANT

I work with a social word, a word that is and is not mine, inherited and always ambiguous, multiform and petrified at the same time. I am

---

Translated by Michael Buzan and Guillermo García-Corales.

submerged in the center of an incomplete landscape, immersed in a work whose only satisfaction consists of complying with my obsession for the word. And on this fringe (on the fringe implied by the word, which is the great literary material), my doing, my political intention (in the sense of my particular literary politics), will be associated with uncertainty. It is a self-imposed voyage whose unstable route ends in a story that, though belonging to me, is another's (and I will lose it again with its publication). It belongs to another, in the first instance, because the language that I inherited belongs to another, provided by an unquestionably social and familial framework — an otherness deepened by the subterfuges and caresses of my own hand, by the wavering of the word that I chose and that, nevertheless, fails to annul the syllable that I should have discarded; the exhaustion of the expression that precedes me; the petrified stability of the only place that it can construct.

But it is an uncertainty that also leads to pleasure: the pleasure of crafting with the word the material setting of a desire for the word; a scene of writing — its grouping, its volume — that appears as a liberation, as a compensation for orality that flees in the extremes of time, subjecting memory to oblivion.

Nevertheless, literary practice requires me to establish another discourse, a cultural discourse that responds for my work. This second discourse, which is founded on the perceptions of the first — on uncertainty — is, of course, useless for comprehending the work itself, for illuminating it (unless we speak of the field of intentions and, perhaps, failures), but it can begin to generate a supplementary word: that of the author and her cultural determination. It is, therefore, a discourse that is avoidable in its reception, yet seems unavoidable in its emission, since it points out, alludes to, or indicates the cultural conditions of the writer's task and its (subjective) perspective inside a social reality. I will speak, therefore, from my position. I will speak from my cultural experience as a Chilean woman writer.

WHAT TO WRITE? WHAT TO PUBLISH?

I think that publishing in Latin America has a double meaning. On one hand, there is the pleasure of a closed writing, obsessed with its own boundaries, a writing protected because of its codes, judged from the verisimilitude of a landscape, and placed in a hierarchy by national customs. On the other hand, it is a writing exposed to the signs of a crisis that is found in the fragmentation of its cultural productions. I refer, and why not, to the sustained detachment of Latin America that diffuses or confuses the role of a language beyond national boundaries — a historic detachment that permits, for example, that certain literary lineaments become central, lineaments created by publishing houses empowered with influence that transcends borders and uses that power to dictate modes of reading while validating certain kinds of writing. This process trims legibility, cutting around the diverse options of writing and through the margin of the discarded, of the enclosed, and permits the stereotyping of literary forms that leads, in some cases, to impoverished ways of reading Latin American literature.

From this perspective, writing in Latin America seems to be an activity whose dominant impulse is literary creation itself and its regional accent; a fixation — in the archaeologic sense — on its own territory and on the impulses contained in that territory, a role that, nevertheless, is reduced by the effects of a sustained (dis)politics that limits its voice, or rather the cultural destiny of that voice, and that interrupts the symbolic flow of the word by denying it a dialog with other writing. An editorial fence that prohibits the deterritorialization of the word.

CONTEXT THAT SPEAKS

Speaking from that fence, from a specific border and as an inhabitant of a continent marked and consigned by its now chronic poverty, I find myself face to face with its changing discursive parameters, such is the mutation of the discourse (at least the implicit discourse) of social reparation into another of an economic and pragmatic character. An economic discourse that brings with it the implantation of an ensemble of social images that dazzle the public, institutionalizing certain privileged images, a certain mode of living — imperatives that are circulated under the mandate of the desire of consumption. Images that appeal to "common sense" (the sense of the same) in order to transform themselves shortly into a "commonplace" or "topoi," which is none other than the marketplace. Images that struggle to construct a (social) body shaped by supply and demand. Bodies publicized by the power of the media (sustained by propaganda and massive buyouts of commercial space).

Though the politics of consumption is not new, what seems new to me is the correlation that this project is achieving in social discourse and political programs in Latin America, generating and auspicating bodies, promoted by industrial "markings" — especially syntactic mark-ings — bodies cut off by the crushing whims of fashion — of the body as fashion — bodies pursued by the words of advertising — in the manner of a slogan — bodies held captive by the promise of a superficial erotic happiness — the eroticism of consumption. This is a "new epoch" for the Latin bodies that recognize their mirror, their face, their pursued identity, their history, in the symmetrical body that the triumphant market offers.

But there is a counterpart to this project: the extended marginality of Latin America that keeps more than half of its population in extreme poverty. This population is condemned in the "new order" to survive without images, to a material habitation without a "commonplace," distanced from the words that name their aesthetics, kept from recog-nizing themselves in cultural production. The concrete marginality of an extensive part of the American population acquires today, through the implantation of "new discourses," a reality that is outside discussion because it is literally located outside any discussion.

This cultural remainder, that omission committed by the domi-nant discourse, which is none other than economic discourse, implies, at the same time, a remainder of language, a paring down of the popular symbolic universe, a clipping of meanings. The minority in extreme poverty is, like all minorities — despite their bruising numbers — condemned to a form of extinction. I refer to a symbolic extinction because their body is made to vanish at the public level, along with their expectations; a symbolic extinction because their cultural future is threatened.

THE FIRST, THE THIRD WORD

The turbulence of the market affects literature. The publishing houses in Latin America, responsible in part for symbolic material, struggle to remain in the "new orders" and, in order to avoid their demise as institutions, seem to promote a literature that constructs and is constructed on the basis of the "common sense" of the end of the century; a literary discourse whose images have the transparency of fashion, self-assured calmness in speech, the linguistic material of the consumer; a literature that is consumed with the vertigo of the last (and only) product; a literature whose story maintains the tone of the "commonplace."

But if Latin America is also marked by its opacity, if its official word is the result of a battle for language, if the memory of its defeat (or of its triumph, according to one's point of view) is the mixing of races (*mestizaje*), if its race is its difference (I speak of a particular facial code), if its regionalization produces the jargon (that ciphered part of a language, its spatial history), then what do you do with the word in the "Third World," its first and only commercial word? I don't know. But this is the dilemma that the literary market promotes today because it is definitely a question of implanting a "new" political project.

THE IMPERATIVE OF THE CONTEXT

What is a possible cultural discourse, then? I think it is one that refers not only to the text but also to the context; a cultural discourse that points out the social conditions of an action, since the result of the action — the book — is subject to the unsteadiness of a project that prescribes — from the shelves of the bookstore — an editorial hierarchy.

Of course, I also feel that a central part of the context is my condition as a woman who writes. Although it does not seem pertinent to repeat here the social reality of Latin American women, I do think it is the right moment to emphasize that a series of omissions, exclusions, and fragmentations remain in effect because of the linearity of a cultural history that assigned unequal roles to the genders, but whose inequality is no less than other unjust social decisions based, for example, on ethnic differences or on the rigid economic categories that give order to public spaces, public destinies.

Therefore, I feel that on our continent a periphery (as opposed to the central power) persists, organized in a determinist fashion. I am thinking, for example, of the impact of a social genealogy or of the ideological conditioning of gender (results of a linear operation with the sexual), organizations that — in my estimation — obviously or subtly, lightly or violently, but always effectively, impinge on concrete habitation. I am thinking of possible hierarchies imposed by the conventions inherent to the system and that permit that system to administer not only the abstraction of civil power but also bodies, desires, and destinies. I am thinking of a system of power already historic in its stubborn behavior and whose struggle seems to be consecrated to the monotonous consummation of that model.

As a counterpart, or at least a counterpoint, in the questioning of conventions, one of the most substantial contributions has been the theory and the actions of feminists. I call it a contribution because it is a way of thinking and acting that has provided tangible amplifications in the psychic and public space of women. Nevertheless, I feel that it is necessary to point out that this proposal originates in countries that are considered to be "developed"; in this sense, we, as members of countries that are colonized or dependent or receivers of "First World" production or productivity, should accept this proposal while maintaining a certain distance, some degree of caution toward its operation, since its hypotheses are delineated, delimited, and attached to a specific reality.

What I am saying does not mean that the dilemma of gender or ethnic divisions can be "regionalized." But it can reflect the "internationalism" of the various categories, a particular method of cultural administration, marked by the profile of history — a history that is perhaps neither more nor less conflictive, but where the weight of signs promotes differences, and not merely differences pertaining to habits or living conditions. Rather, I want to express that the extended lack of an existence (such as in the case of Latin America) shapes a specific psyche, intricate social relations, and desires concocted in a world ruled by the work of artisans — a world disintegrated by technological production.

Even so, it seems that feminist theory has become one of the contemporary forms of thought that has most strongly launched the questioning of the codes of power. Its strength and efficacy, without a doubt, are related to the reason brought by its demand. And this bruising questioning becomes part of the theoretical field, along with psychoanalysis, political theory, and even economic theory, reshaping thought circuits, revealing the excessive, arbitrary nature of ideologic constructions and placing gender at one of the poles of thought.

On the other hand, feminist action — I refer to concrete international organizations — has managed to create an interesting dialog with the institutions that administer power, thus interjecting minimum criteria of equality into the public and familial actions of women.

Beyond the crises that international feminist organizations have suffered, such as increasing fragmentation and polarization within their ranks, or the weakening of their demands due to the inevitable political posturing that allows their conversations to continue, and this side of the resulting dismantling of the organic body (a dismantling that turns out to be understandable if one considers feminist activity as a critical space that seeks to reshape the administration of power), the gains already achieved are, at least for the present, undeniable.

One way a woman connects with reality becomes evident with maternity — a peculiarity of the female body. It is, perhaps, a joyful relationship with the power of the body that "creates" incessantly. And through this "creation," Latin women are defined by their multiple gestations. Without going into the ideological conditioning inherent in maternity, nor in the series of social problems associated with overpopulation, I would like to take note of the moment of gestation, of the authority of a body, thinking of that body as a creative challenge; a body that is especially active among those social sectors with the greatest needs.

But thinking of that body implies that one must establish a reflection, a reading and a revision of history itself, so that it does not ignore those other bodies, those which are subjected to negative pressures by the dominant forces. If, at the symbolic level, the feminine is that which is oppressed by the central power, it seems legitimate to extend that category to include all those groups which share that condition, since the condition of abandonment — be it at the symbolic or material level — is not unique to the social and biological body of women.

I envision a joint theory and action that, in the feminist manner, encompasses and extends thought and action toward an interdisciplinary plan that provides greater means of perception to the social future.

LITERATURE AND THE FEMININE

The effects of feminism are beginning to appear in the literary field in Latin America. Terms such as "feminine literature" or "women's literature" or "feminist literature" are terms with which we, women who write, are becoming familiar; terms restored through the discompensation of a literary history that has been organized in a centralist way of writing produced by men, a literary history that has been affected by a scarce and always peripheral writing by women.

The implementation of these terms has created an interesting and valuable critical and theoretical discourse, broadening the readings of and perspectives on literary works. This is an area of thought production that, while examining the writing of women, brings new criteria to follow the orders and disorders of a lexicon, the visual figure that presents the subjectivity or the eroticism of the work on a textual body. This production is what seems to me truly relevant in that it demands a more exhaustive and complex questioning of this group of texts.

Nevertheless, I feel I should point out the insistence of certain simplifying operations that reiterate — in another way — symptoms of exclusion. I believe the use of the term "feminine" is abused when it establishes a field of competition among (women's) writings, and in this dispute for hegemony, the other hegemony — the traditional one — remains untouched. This is a procedure that through sexual division, though it does not hide it, does confine women's writing to one privileged reference: being a woman, thus reducing the intensity of meanings carried by the textuality of a literary work.

I believe — and I admit my own lack of specialization in the field — that writing is a social instrument, an instrument that historically has been employed by men and, in literature, that possibly has meant a great reduction of sensitivity for the suspiciously scarce presence of women. But think of the potential: these oppressed writings could have made a contribution by altering, enlarging, or modifying the center, producing perhaps a tremor or a slight unsettling of meanings in literary production, energizing the movement that guarantees its existence. But, of course, this intention could be in the writing of a man as well as in that of a woman.

What seems vital to me is dealing with the amplitude of literary codes more than with the obvious thematic content of a work. In other words, I do not believe that being a woman is enough to guarantee a worthwhile literature. In the same way, it seems certain to me that some of the literature produced by men is merely an indulgence to the market. I am fascinated by a literature that questions its own zones of production and that, in the symbolic order, enlarges its meanings. I perceive literary diversity, as diverse as the conflicts and the modes of production.

And if the ostensible bonds of social order that restrict the woman writer seem to me repudiable, my gaze continues to be upon the variety of production and the fundamental aesthetic orders that determine the politics of writing.

Mario Vargas Llosa on D. H. Lawrence: An Interview

FLETCHER FAIREY, *Chapel Hill, North Carolina*

The Peruvian Mario Vargas Llosa, author of ten novels and various collections of literary essays (the latest of which is entitled *La verdad de las mentiras*, 1990), made a trip from Boulder, Colorado, to the D. H. Lawrence ranch in Taos, New Mexico, in April 1991. On that occasion, Mr. Vargas Llosa shared his ideas about Lawrence's work and his ranch, about art and pornography, and provided some background on his own latest novel, *In Praise of the Stepmother* (1990).

FAIREY: I know that you have wanted to make this trip for some time. Why was a visit to a place where D. H. Lawrence spent a few years of his life, and where his ashes now reside, so attractive to you?

VARGAS LLOSA: I am a bit of a literary fetishist. That is, I'm intrigued by the places and objects of writers' experience. Especially in Lawrence's fiction personal experience was important, and it's fascinating to see firsthand a part of his life.

FAIREY: Have you had a lifelong fascination with Lawrence's work? What were the circumstances of your first contact with his fiction?

VARGAS LLOSA: I first read Lawrence as a university student in Lima in the 1950s. I read his novels *Sons and Lovers*, *Women in Love*, and *Lady Chatterley's Lover*. I especially enjoyed his essays on American writers.

FAIREY: Did you read these works in English, or were there Spanish translations available?

VARGAS LLOSA: Victoria O'Campo's publishing house, Sur, had many of Lawrence's and other European writers' works translated and published. I believe Borges translated *The White Peacock*. This was an important publishing house for writers of my generation. Therefore, these first readings in the 1950s were of translations.

FAIREY: There were subsequent readings of the English texts?

VARGAS LLOSA: Yes. In fact, in London in the 1960s I read *Lady Chatterley's Lover* in English, which improved the book considerably.

FAIREY: Was there anything in particular which initiated this return to Lawrence?

VARGAS LLOSA: I came back to Lawrence after reading F. R. Leavis' book on the English writer, a book which I found interesting but arbitrary, especially his fascination with the moral goals of Lawrence's work. So I read Leavis' book along with the corresponding Lawrence novels. I had also read a wonderful essay on Lawrence by André Malraux.

FAIREY: You are very acquainted with Lawrence's work, and I know that Carlos Fuentes, Octavio Paz, and numerous other Latin American writers have also had interest in this writer. Why was your generation so attracted to Lawrence?

VARGAS LLOSA: We read Lawrence primarily because he was a rebel. There was a mystique about Lawrence because of the censorship of *Lady Chatterley's Lover*. We read Henry Miller for the same reasons.

FAIREY: It's also interesting that he was a widely read and translated author in Latin America because some of his books, like *The Plumed Serpent*, seem to reveal a complete lack of cultural sensitivity.

VARGAS LLOSA: *The Plumed Serpent* is Lawrence's worst novel. It's a failure because it shows a total incapacity to understand Mexico. The writing in that novel is kitsch. Lawrence didn't understand anything about Mexico. Instead he fabricated something about this different world. However, you can compare this novel with other great novels, like *Women in Love* and *Sons and Lovers*, and some short stories because it shows a fascination with esoteric worlds.

FAIREY: I'm not sure that I understand exactly what you mean by "esoteric worlds" in Lawrence's work.

VARGAS LLOSA: Lawrence is interesting because he discovered how to incorporate Freud's theories on the unconscious and sexuality in his fiction. Lawrence dealt with his own secret sexual problems and wrote with frankness and courage. This made him a very different kind of author.

FAIREY: I know that William Faulkner was a great model for you. In fact, you have referred to Faulkner as the first writer you read with pen in hand, analyzing his narrative techniques. From what you've said, it appears that Lawrence was not that type of writer for you.

VARGAS LLOSA: No, Lawrence was not a model for my writing; I never read him with pen in hand. His narrative technique was conventional and he was not very innovative, although his language was quite interesting.

FAIREY: Nevertheless, are there any points of contact between these two writers, who were contemporaries?

VARGAS LLOSA: Lawrence was not unlike Faulkner in his reaction against intellectualism. Both felt that intellectualism killed life and pleasure, that it took away from a rich and fruitful life. They both stressed the idea that theory and intellectualism suppressed spontaneity, which is the life-giving force.

FAIREY: Where would you place Lawrence in light of two other central writers of his time, James Joyce and Virginia Woolf?

VARGAS LLOSA: Lawrence's work is very unequal. He wrote some disastrous things, like *The Plumed Serpent* and *Kangaroo*, while everything that Woolf wrote, for instance, is interesting. And Joyce was nothing less than a genius. So, I would have to say that Lawrence is less important. Also, while one is struck by the formalistic innovation of Woolf and Joyce, Lawrence's work, as I've said, is more conventional. But Lawrence stands out because of his messianic attitude as a prophet of a new religion, a religion of sex, pleasure, and nature.

FAIREY: Yes, there is certainly a good bit of sex in Lawrence's fiction. He had problems with the censors in his time, and even today one is struck by the erotic nature of his work. As critics, we cerebral types often consider sex in fiction at best an example of other conflicts or themes in the work; at worst cheap pornography. What important role does sex play in Lawrence's work, your work, or in fiction in general?

VARGAS LLOSA: Sexual experience is a central part of life and for an artist to ignore that is inappropriate. Especially the novel, as total representation, should not ignore the sexual, the sensual, and the erotic. It is only if these elements completely dominate a work that their use becomes mechanical and something resembling pornography.

FAIREY: But where can one draw the line between the sexual-sensual-erotic work and the pornographic work?

VARGAS LLOSA: The line between these limits is fine; it is a formal matter. If the structure of a work treats these matters with sensibility and a formal acumen, then that work transcends pornography. While the sex in Lawrence is prudent and orthodox, as opposed to the baroque and torturous sex in Faulkner, it is often hyperbolic. This caused problems. But it was not gratuitous sex: it was expressed very beautifully, with a stylistic excellence not found in pornography.

FAIREY: So how would you explain Lawrence's problems with the censors?

VARGAS LLOSA: Lawrence lived in a world of repression, almost puritan in tone. And Lawrence, in some sense, expressed the religion of the body, a revolutionary and courageous stance to take in his time. Frieda, his second wife, appears to be the one who converted Lawrence to this corporeal religion.

FAIREY: As we talk about the sensual and erotic nature of Lawrence's fiction, I cannot help but think of your latest novel, *In Praise of the Stepmother*, which has been described by some as an erotic novel. How did you conceive this work?

VARGAS LLOSA: The original idea was to create a book with the Peruvian painter Fernando Szyszlo: I was going to write the text and he was going to do the illustrations. Originally, we conceived of this as a joint project. Unfortunately, we were never able to coordinate our ideas on this book, although the concept of relating paintings and fiction continued to intrigue me. That is why the language is so visual and descriptive. For the first time, I did use *langage précieux*. In other words, the language in this novel is not so transparent; rather, it is a presence by itself.

FAIREY: So meditating on these paintings, which are actually reproduced in the text, helped you construct a pictorial language?

VARGAS LLOSA: Well, the fact of the matter is that I did not write this novel while looking at the paintings, but rather used paintings that were already in my memory, residing there for whatever reason. They must have been important to me or I would have forgotten them. I used my memory to fantasize rather than to meditate. I wasn't trying to be accurate; instead, I tried to improvise freely.

FAIREY: Another outstanding aspect of Lawrence's work is his dedication to the novel as a supreme form of art. In some of his critical works he points out that the novel is the best way to avoid absolutes. He writes, "The novel is the highest form of human expression so far attained. Why? Because it is so incapable of the absolute." Likewise many of your novels have been dedicated, in part, to exposing the hypocrisies and the dangers of fanaticism. Is the novel the most appropriate genre to express this interest in nonabsolutes?

VARGAS LLOSA: The novel is a literary genre which needs to express the relationship of people among people. While poetry is an expression of the individual, the novel is never solipsistic. Rather, it deals with human relations. To write a novel you need this kind of pluralistic vision of problems and attitudes. The novel is related to history and social issues; it is a genre which can absorb other genres, like poetry and theater. It is an ambitious process. But the novel, in order to succeed, cannot be exclusively concerned with history. It is an artistic form and must add something to the living world. That is the ambiguity of the novel: if it deals only with the past, it is a failed novel, for it must be the creation of something new. It must be the product of fantasy, imagination, and obsessions. The great novelists integrate history and social experience with a new and totally inventive element.

FAIREY: What is your favorite novel by Lawrence?

VARGAS LLOSA: *The Rainbow* stands out as the best in my memory. It is a rich novel, full of diversity. *Sons and Lovers* is another great work. *The Plumed Serpent* was his worst, and even *Lady Chatterley's Lover* was somewhat of a failure because it is a bit naive, focusing on a revival of pagan desires in middle-class English society. The pagan love scenes are a bit ridiculous, even though they include some powerful images. But in all of Lawrence's work, without having to agree with him, you can judge him with sympathy.

FAIREY: In your readings, what is the source of this sympathy?

VARGAS LLOSA: It is obvious that Lawrence had a fear of industrial society which he felt could destroy some of the most valuable aspects of humanity. Therefore, he focused on the natural man. You could say that Lawrence was a reactionary, but his revelation of the dehumanizing process has been justified by what is happening today in the world. You could actually do an ecological reading of Lawrence without any problems. Another essential aspect of Lawrence's philosophy is his desire to understand and see different cultures. And even though many of these projects failed, you can still safely say that Lawrence was not ethnocentric.

FAIREY: Now that you have seen the D. H. Lawrence ranch, what are your impressions?

VARGAS LLOSA: It's a very beautiful place. I can see how Lawrence would have liked it very much. For a man who was fascinated and impressed by natural forces, this place is perfect. Lawrence had a passion for the preindustrial world: he saw in what some consider progress a force transforming man into machine. Ah, but here in this beautiful setting, under this immense sky, you can feel the natural forces which Lawrence found more interesting and more humanizing.